OUT
OF MY
LEAGUE

BOOKS BY GEORGE PLIMPTON

The Rabbit's Umbrella • *Out of My League*
Paper Lion • *The Bogey Man* • *Mad Ducks and Bears*
American Journey: The Times of Robert Kennedy
(with Jean Stein) • *One for the Record* • *One More July*
Shadow Box • *Pierre's Book* (with Pierre Etchebaster)
A Sports Bestiary (with Arnold Roth)
Edie: An American Biography (with Jean Stein)
Sports! (with Neil Leifer) • *Fireworks: A History and Celebration*
Open Net • *D.V.* (with Diana Vreeland and Christopher Hemphill)
The Curious Case of Sidd Finch • *The X Factor*
The Best of Plimpton • *Truman Capote* • *Ernest Shackleton*
Chronicles of Courage (with Jean Kennedy Smith)
The Man in the Flying Lawn Chair

EDITED BY GEORGE PLIMPTON

Writers at Work: The Paris Review Interviews, vols. 1–9
The American Literary Anthology, vols. 1–3
Poets at Work: The Paris Review Interviews
Beat Writers at Work: The Paris Review Interviews
Women Writers at Work: The Paris Review Interviews
Playwrights at Work: The Paris Review Interviews
Latin American Writers at Work: The Paris Review Interviews
The Writer's Chapbook • *The Paris Review Anthology*
The Paris Review Book of Heartbreak, Madness, etc.
The Norton Book of Sports • *As Told at the Explorers Club:
More Than Fifty Gripping Tales of Adventure* • *Home Run*

OUT
OF MY
LEAGUE

THE CLASSIC ACCOUNT OF AN AMATEUR'S ORDEAL IN PROFESSIONAL BASEBALL

GEORGE PLIMPTON

Little, Brown and Company
New York   Boston   London

Little, Brown and Company
Hachette Book Group
1290 Avenue of the Americas, New York, NY 10104
littlebrown.com

Originally published by Harper and Brothers, 1961
First Little, Brown edition, April 2016

Little, Brown and Company is a division of Hachette Book Group, Inc. The Little, Brown name and logo are trademarks of Hachette Book Group, Inc.

The publisher is not responsible for websites (or their content) that are not owned by the publisher.

The Hachette Speakers Bureau provides a wide range of authors for speaking events. To find out more, go to hachettespeakersbureau.com or call (866) 376-6591.

ISBN 978-0-316-28454-7
LCCN 2015952969

10 9 8 7 6 5 4 3 2 1

RRD-C

Printed in the United States of America

I do not think that they will sing to me.

—T. S. Eliot, *The Love Song of J. Alfred Prufrock*

Foreword

by Jane Leavy

The afternoon that George Plimpton first humiliated himself in the name of participatory journalism, I was throwing a tennis ball at the garage door of my childhood home 21.7 miles and a world away from Yankee Stadium, where I, too, longed to pitch. When he took the mound with a borrowed glove in a motley approximation of a uniform to face American and National League All-Star teams led by Willie Mays and Mickey Mantle, I was toeing an imaginary pitching rubber, trying to decide how to pitch to the Say Hey Kid.

I was seven years old, a first-grader, exuberantly exercising my imagination in which I was Ryne Duren, the Yankees' myopic relief pitcher, heaving a final warm-up pitch all the way to the backstop just to put the fear of God in Willie. Plimpton was the thirty-one-year-old editor of the *Paris Review* with the means and the moxie to make imagination real.

Toots Shor, the bon-vivant saloonkeeper, made the necessary introductions. *Sports Illustrated* provided the financial backing. Armed with little more than muscle memory and chutzpah, Plimpton contrived to pitch to the major league All-Stars prior to a previously scheduled exhibition game. The winning team would split $1,000.

The stadium announcer introduced him to 20,000 witnesses in the stands as George Prufrock. As in T. S. Eliot's "The Love Song of J. Alfred Prufock"—a middle-aged man with an "overwhelming" question he can't bring himself to ask.

Like Prufrock, Plimpton had a question: what's it like to stand 60 feet 6 inches away from Willie Mays with a ball in your hand? Unlike Prufrock, he was determined to act, determined to get an answer to his question.

He approached his task with cheerful WASP sangfroid, given that he hadn't picked up a baseball in ten years. At least I would have brought a glove. Gazing from the dugout at the vastness of the ballpark before taking the mound—five years later Sandy Koufax would say it was like pitching in the Grand Canyon—Plimpton mused: "For me the future was uncertain and perhaps the best I could hope for was survival without shame."

Which is one way to describe the human condition.

Plimpton wasn't the first author to essay participatory sportswriting; he was just the best. Mark Twain was paid twenty dollars by the *Sacramento Union* to attempt what was called "surf-bathing" in 1866. Following the example of the naked locals, he paddled a wooden surfboard out to the break in Hawaiian waters and immediately wiped out. "The board struck the shore in three-quarters of a second, without any cargo, and I struck the bottom about the same time," Twain reported.

Twenty-some years earlier, Charles Dickens wrote about hiking through snow and ice to the summit of Mount Vesuvius in the dark—his wife, daughter, and a rotund Italian he called Mr.

Pickle of Portici schlepped aloft in litters by guides who should have known better. Up, up, up they went until it seemed they were "toiling to the summit of an antediluvian Twelfth-cake," he wrote in *Pictures from Italy*.

Determined to look into the molten maw of the fuming mountain, Dickens crawled through the ashes to gaze "into the Hell of boiling fire below." After which he and his guides came "rolling down; blackened, and singed, and scorched, and hot, and giddy," each with "his dress alight in half-a-dozen places."

Plimpton names Paul Gallico as his inspiration. In 1923, Gallico was a cub reporter in the sports department of the *New York Daily News*. Hired as a favor to his late father-in-law by publisher and film buff Joseph Patterson, he had lost his first job as movie critic for having exercised his critical faculties too liberally. "Fire him," Captain Patterson said.

The managing editor saw something in him and buried him in the sports department without a byline. That August, Gallico was sent to cover Jack Dempsey's training camp in Saratoga Springs, New York, as the heavyweight champ prepared to meet Luis Ángel Firpo, "the Wild Bull of the Pampas," in September.

It was there that Gallico conceived the notion that it was impossible to write "graphically and understandingly" about a heavyweight fight without having gone a round with said heavyweight. He wanted to know what thoughts go through a man's mind when he can't think at all.

He approached Dempsey with the proposition that they spar a round. "What's the matter, son?" Dempsey asked. "Don't your editor like you no more?"

Gallico left the ring bloodied, addled, and informed. "It

seems I had gone to an expert for tuition," he wrote when he came sufficiently to his senses, enough anyway to get to his typewriter. Knocked out cold and he still made his deadline. (Dempsey would have hired a ghostwriter.)

It was Gallico's first byline as a sportswriter. A year later, Patterson made him sports editor.

I never tried my hand at participatory sportswriting. By the time I was of age, the era had passed. I played tennis with Billie Jean King in my stocking feet once. At the time, she was my boss and I never wrote about it. The closest I ever came to a Plimpton moment was a scheduled first pitch at a spring-training game. I worked for three months to get my arm in shape. No way was I going to be one of those wimpy girls standing on the grass between the mound and the plate, giggling at my own ineptitude. When I learned that Sandy Koufax was going to be in attendance, I asked if he'd relieve me in a pinch. "No fuckin' way, Leavy," he replied, which left me with a slight approximation of the loneliness Plimpton felt on the Yankee Stadium mound. In my last bullpen session, my catcher clanked a throw off my kneecap, sending me to the disabled list before I could set foot on the field.

Training and timing consigned me to the sidelines: an outsider, which is, after all, what a reporter is supposed to be. I never felt an overwhelming need to get punched in the nose, nor do I believe personal experience is a requirement for writing "graphically and understandingly" about pitching, punching, or, for that matter, the presidency. No one says you have to be queen for a day in order to write about the queen. Even Plimpton couldn't have gotten that gig.

In today's bloated sports economy, he couldn't have gotten the gig at Yankee Stadium either. There's no way any prima-donna athlete on any professional team will do anything for the $125 promised each of the victorious All-Stars.

One of the many seductive charms of reading *Out of My League,* an excerpt of which was first published in the April 10, 1961, issue of *Sports Illustrated* under the title "Dream of Glory on the Mound," is to return to a cheaper, kinder, less self-serious time when access to professional athletes didn't require a security clearance and ballplayers tolerated—and occasionally indulged—authors with a Walter Mitty complex.

Plimpton hadn't thought to engage an umpire. Nor had it crossed his mind that major league hitters weren't going to swing at just anything, not when money was involved. They were going to be *selective,* make him *come to them,* which, alas, he could not do. He threw seventy-some pitches to the first seven batters he faced, twenty-three of them to Ernie Banks, the National League's Most Valuable Player. By way of perspective: a Boston Braves pitcher named Red Barrett threw fifty-eight pitches in a one-hour-and-fifteen-minute *complete game* victory in 1944.

In his exhaustion, Plimpton lost control of his fastball, his fingers, and then his mind, which decamped to a high "observation booth"—the press box, perhaps?—somewhere above his disintegrating physical self. As he hallucinated and dissociated—the narrative voice careening between the first and second person—his inner voice began talking out loud in a po' white-trash Southern accent never heard at Phillips Exeter, Harvard, or Cambridge.

Midway through Plimpton's eighth hitter, Ralph Houk, the

Yankees coach— known as "Major" for his valor at the Battle of the Bulge—invoked the mercy rule. Ambling to the mound, he took the ball. Shell-shocked, Plimpton staggered to the bench, where he learned that players in the American League dugout were making book on when he'd keel over.

It was a precedent-setting appearance for literature and baseball. "Driven to the showers before the game had even started," the Yankee trainer said when he saw Plimpton stumble across the locker room.

In its brief recap of the exhibition game the next morning, the *New York Times* discreetly omitted Plimpton's pitching line.

Author's Note

Out of My League was the first of my participatory journalistic books (*Paper Lion*, *The Bogey Man*, *Shadow Box*, *Open Net*). With its publication came the inevitable comparisons to Walter Mitty, which was not quite accurate since James Thurber's memorable character always succeeded in his daydreams, whereas from *Out of My League* on I have suffered a steady series of humiliations at the higher levels of football, hockey, golf, and so on. What happened to me is bound to happen when an amateur is thrown into the company of professional athletes. It is inevitable.

Ernest Hemingway seized on this. I had sent him the galleys of the book in the hope he would provide a quote, a blurb. Actually I was brazen enough to ask him for an introduction! Not long before the book went to press, a telegram arrived from the Mayo Clinic where Hemingway was being treated for depression. He had provided a blurb. In it was the lovely line about what I had gone through being "the dark side of the moon of Walter Mitty."

The publishers slapped the quote on the jacket, the letters of Hemingway's name in oversize capitals, and I have no doubt that the success of the book was helped immeasurably by its being there.

I have a poet friend who is opposed to blurbs—believing that readers ought to be able to make up their minds about a book without being influenced by a quote that has probably been induced by a trade-off—one writer promising to praise another if the favor can be returned. He even dislikes the word itself and thinks it should only be used to describe the sound a scuba diver makes when close to drowning.

I hold no brief on this matter, one way or the other. But I'm awfully glad that telegram arrived from Rochester!

OUT
OF MY
LEAGUE

CHAPTER 1

On a late summer's day I was in New York's Yankee Stadium, up there on a weekday, and able to get a seat in the sun behind the third-base dugout. I don't ever remember being as close to a major league baseball diamond. The players were only yards away. You could see their jaws working on chaws or gum, and every once in a while you'd hear a snatch of conversation.

The game started, and along about the fifth inning Mickey Mantle stepped up and hit a home run over the right-field wall. I watched the high, long flight of the ball, and then looked at the pitcher. He was peering into the depths of his glove—a rather proud figure, I thought, trying his best to snub that last minute and Mantle's explosive force from existence. But he couldn't do it. At the last second, just as Mantle was trotting in from third, he peeked up from his glove and took one sorrowful glance at the heavy-striding Yankee whose power only seconds before had made his ears, in Paul Gallico's fine phrase, feel "long and furry."

The pitcher got through the inning without further difficulty. After the last out he came walking in toward the third-base dugout, his head down, what I could see of it as bland as a vicar's — not a twitch in it — and then suddenly as he reached the top step of the dugout, just a couple of yards from me, his face contorted and I heard him shout at his teammates, "D'ja get a load of *that*? That crumbum! Threw him a—" and then his head ducked down into the dugout. I envied him — even his difficulty with Mantle. I leaned far out of my seat trying to hear — hoping to get some indication of what it was like to face Mantle from the pitcher's mound, to see him begin to uncoil his swing at a pitch, and yet I knew that no matter how articulate the pitcher, still it wouldn't be enough. It was something you had to experience yourself to know truly, and as I sat there in the summer sun I suddenly began to wonder, timidly, if there wasn't some way of climbing the field-box railings and getting out there to the pitcher's mound to try it myself — under major league conditions — just to see what it was like and how I'd get along.

In Spain they have a word for a fellow struck by this sort of foolishness. An *espontáneo* they call him — the haunted young man who starts moving down from his cheap seat toward the bullring, perching on the end of the seats, upturning the wine flask and hissing a fine stream of wine into the back of his throat, then moving on down until with a sudden rush he drops into the *callejón,* vaults the *barrera,* and runs across the open sand of the bullring, perhaps with a cape he's smuggled in under his shirt but more likely with a rag of a raincoat held before him, moving jerkily but quickly toward the bull — he hasn't much time — and then with a great wash of noise he's noticed; everyone sees him — the crowd, the matador and his cuadrilla, the bull. He'll have less than a minute to perform before the bull is distracted from him, and if he survives, and even if his feet betray him before the bull's rush, he'll hear what he's done it for—the roar of applause in his ears as he's hustled off, given the bum's rush with such dispatch that with his feet an inch or so above the ground he jiggles between the hurrying ring attendants like a loosely stuffed straw man.

This sort of exhibitionism is unknown in America. We are a vociferous people, to be sure, and a good hand-cupped yell in support of the team of his choice will lift a man, red-necked, two or three inches out of his seat, and his neighbors out of theirs if his vocal effort is startling enough, but then invariably he sags back down when his breath is done and looks around for the hot-dog vendor. Sometimes, of course, a drunk will take the field, and once or twice a summer at Yankee Stadium a quartet of men in tight trousers and white shirts drop over the low right-field fence with a banner bearing a long political message they intend to display to the stands. They never rehearse, apparently; despite frantic maneuvering on the field they rarely get their bedsheeted banner spread out more than to show a word or two of their slo-gan, *cuba sí*..., usually upside down, and then the police move for them. Entwined in their sheets like Laocoön and his sons in the serpents' grip, they're collared easily and bundled out—rushed for the exits past outfielders, ignoring the disturbance, tossing a baseball back and forth to keep their arms limber.

These men are Latins, who take the dividing line between spectator and playing field very lightly. In Southern Europe and the South American countries a triple strand of barbed wire is often put around the field to keep the citizens out of the soccer matches; even so the referees run nervously about their duties, keeping an eye cocked to the sidelines for the sudden flow of spectators overrunning the fence to avenge a wrong decision with quick violence.

In the Northern countries only the Welsh seem to have similar tendencies. Like the Latins, they have big, fine voices, and at heart the Welshman is a performer. You see him erupt onto the field during the great soccer and rugger internationals abroad, usually appearing just before the game starts to get the undivided attention of the massed tiers of spectators. He will come across the sidelines wearing a long overcoat, like a circus clown's, a woolen scarf looped round his neck, and in his hand he carries a leek, the onion-like plant which is the national emblem of the Welsh, waving this thing, a forlorn figure down there but strutting cockily and buoyed along by the vibrant thunder of patriotic songs from the Welsh stands, a sound you hear blocks from the stadium and which from your seat is so powerful and stirring that the comic cavorting of the distant figure comes as a relief. The police gather and go after him. They move at a slow walk. But in their numbers they move across the field in long, treacherous coils like an anaconda — escaped once or twice by the taunting Welshman but not for long: a quick constriction and they've got him. The leek flails briefly and feebly, and the Welshman is lifted quickly off the field by two bobbies who support him between them gingerly and with the disdain of two butlers removing a miscreant six-year-old. The Welsh spectators yell their chagrin. But then another Welshman jumps out onto the field and starts that same cocky walk, the long woolen scarf with the Welsh colors trailing, and when the police enfold him he'll have his successors. The Welsh are a hard people to keep in their seats — the *espontáneos* of the north.

Comparatively, in America we are content to stay behind the box railings. I recall a middle-aged man, an Illinois alumnus, who rushed onto the football field and tried to tackle Michigan's great Tommy Harmon just at the end of a long touchdown run. But he did it, apparently, not to show off, or out of temper even, but simply out of exasperation, and a truly overwhelming desire to help his alma mater stop the brilliant halfback. He was unsuccessful, missed his tackle and fell sprawling, and I remember the news photos of him—a portly man in an overcoat sadly getting up from his knees.

Among American sportswriters, however, there was one famous *espontáneo:* Paul Gallico, at one time the highest-paid sportswriter in New York, a big burly bespectacled man with a stooped but powerful build, and quick reflexes, good enough with an épée in his hand to win fencing championships. In the days before he gave up sports reporting to write about snow geese, and charwomen in the boutique of Christian Dior's fashion house, Gallico believed that it was helpful for a sportswriter to have played or at least attempted to play the games he would be called upon to describe in his stories—if only that he would gain a better understanding of what athletes were up against and what they were trying to do. In a book entitled *Farewell to Sport* Gallico devoted one chapter—called "The Feel"—to some of his experiences. He described, among other things, catching Herb Pennock's curveball, playing tennis against Vinnie Richards, golf with Bobby Jones, and what it was like coming down the Olympic ski run six thousand feet above Garmisch—quite a feat considering he had been on skis only once before in his life. Whichever sport he tried was at the championship level, except water polo, which he refused to do at all. In his primal and tremendous curiosity with regard to sensation—to see "what it was like"—it wasn't enough to climb into the boxing ring and be hit by a fair middleweight. In 1922, in Saratoga Springs, fresh out of Columbia, Gallico arranged to climb into the ring and box one round with heavyweight champion Jack Dempsey, then preparing for his fight with Luis Firpo. Dempsey stalked him, whacked him down to the canvas, and when Gallico left the ring he was shaking, bleeding slightly from his mouth, rosin dust on his trunks, his head singing, and, as he wrote, "knowing all there was to know about being hit in the ring. It seems I had gone to an expert for tuition."

When I came home that day from Yankee Stadium, I wondered if it would be possible to emulate Gallico, yet go further by writing at length and in depth about each sport and what it was like to participate. The impulse to try kept nagging. But what had set me off—the possibility of playing in a major league baseball game—seemed so remote and preposterous that, having caught briefly on the edge of my mind, the whole idea would have vanished in a day or so if I hadn't read a news story the next morning which reported that after the World Series, then over a month away, an exhibition game was scheduled in Yankee Stadium between an All-Star team from the American League captained by Mickey Mantle, and a National League team led by Willie Mays. The rosters were impressive; just about everybody who had played in the official All-Star game earlier that summer was included: Whitey Ford, Nellie Fox, Billy Pierce, Harvey Kuenn, Billy Martin, and Frank Malzone of the American League, and, among others, on the National League team, Frank Thomas, Bill Mazeroski, Bob Friend, Richie Ashburn, Gil Hodges, and Ernie Banks. I read the short announcement and the list of players, wondering if the occasion would give me a chance to participate. It was billed as an All-Star game, but being off-season and an exhibition, perhaps it would be relaxed and informal enough so that I might be allowed in to pitch an inning. It seemed unlikely, but for a few days I kept toying with the notion of doing something about it until I began to be plagued by those half-forgotten boyhood dreams of heroics on the major league baseball diamond, so many of them flooding my mind that finally I took the newspaper clipping and went to see Sid James, the editor of *Sports Illustrated*.

At that time the magazine was situated in Rockefeller Center. James had an office on the southwest corner, and past him, as he rocked and swayed in a swivel chair which squeaked badly, you could see down the length of 48th Street—clear to the Hudson River on a good day. I knew James well. I had done work for him previously. When I gave him the clipping, he pushed back his swivel chair to give himself turning room and with a shove of his foot began to dip and revolve, only briefly, because the article was short, and then he pulled himself back up to the desk with a sudden squeal of swivel-chair wheels. He said: "Well, sure, but what's in this for us?"

"The fact of the matter is," I said, "that I'd like to *play* in that game. I'm a pitcher. I want to pitch in it."

"I see," he said slowly. His chair was now absolutely still.

"Mind you, I want to write about what happens," I said defensively. "I mean that's the purpose of the project."

"Sure."

"I've no pretensions about any sudden career as a pitcher," I assured him. "I mean I'm not trying to use my...ah...vague connections with *Sports Illustrated* to wangle a big-league tryout, or anything like that."

"That would be a novel idea," he said. "Incidentally, you can pitch, can't you?"

"I pitched at school," I told him, "and at college a bit, and once or twice in the army. But the point is," I went on, "that I would pitch not as a hotshot—that'd be a different story—but as a guy who's average, really, a sort of Mr. Everybody, the sort who thinks he's a fair athlete, a good tennis player, but always finds himself put out in the second round of the club tournament by the sandy-haired member who wears a hearing aid."

The author pitching as a youngster on the St. Bernard's School team. (*Plimpton Estate*)

"I see," he said.

There was a leather sofa behind me and I sat down in it. "James Thurber," I said obliquely, "once wrote that the majority of American males put themselves to sleep by striking out the batting order of the New York Yankees. That's my fellow, you see, lying there staring at the bedroom ceiling...the bases loaded, and he's imagining himself coming in from the bullpen, when downstairs the screen door squeaks open and smacks to, and who comes charging up the stairs and into the bedroom but Casey Stengel, there in the flesh, you see...plunging through the bedroom door and leaning over the bed to shout at our fellow there that he'd a hunch, a *big* hunch, the biggest hunch of his managing career, namely, that our fellow was going to solve his relief pitching problem, and that he'd better get up to the stadium and suit up the next afternoon...and our fellow—despite his protestations, despite the fact that he hadn't *gripped* a ball in ten years—did take a taxi the next day, and there he is in the dugout trying to spit neatly between his shoes like everyone else, and in the middle of the game sent in by Stengel with the bases loaded, just like his dream, but it isn't, you see...he's really up there on the mound, sweating, the ball as unfamiliar in his hand as something dead...and what I want to write about is what happens to him..."

"Well, that's vivid enough," said James. "Frankly it's the sort of nightmare thing we should hope never happens to anyone we know."

"I was exaggerating, perhaps," I said.

"Lord," said James. "The thought of Stengel leaning over a bed and shouting about a big hunch."

"An exaggeration," I said.

He pushed back his chair and began to swoop and revolve in it, the springs squeaking violently under him. "Quite a project," he said finally. "And you're willing to be that fool guinea pig? Go up there and pitch?"

"Well, I can try," I said. "If it works out—the article I mean—then perhaps I could do some more sports: tennis with Pancho Gonzalez, boxing with Archie Moore, football, chess, and so forth, and golf with Snead or Hogan..."

James suddenly came forward in his chair. "You know that's interesting what Thurber writes," he said. "It's an awful commentary on the American male—to think he has his mind on such things—but let me tell you what I often find myself doing in bed at three a.m." He leaned forward, peering past me into the anteroom as if to make sure no one would overhear. *"I sink these long, these incredibly long putts,"* he whispered. He didn't play a full eighteen holes, I was to understand—the action all took place on one immense green. The pleasure came in preparation: reading the green, testing the wind, endless waggling with the putter, and then finally executing the crisp stroke—the ball traveling smoothly over an eternity of green before dropping into the cup with a distant but authoritative rattle....

James paused, and I think if only briefly he was watching a golf ball start to roll across the scope of his inner mind. But then he picked up a pencil and tapped it sharply on the desk. "Well," he said. "I think the project sounds fine, sounds OK. You just go ahead, and when you think you need us, we'll do what we can to help."

I could hear a rustling of papers in the anteroom and the whispering of secretaries which indicated my time was up.

"I don't see why it can't be arranged," he said. "Seems to me," he continued as I stood up, "that your big problem isn't going to be arranging these...er...matches, or writing about what you go through, but getting through everything in one piece...in a word: survival. I would advise getting in shape."

CHAPTER 2

The problem of arranging for my appearance on the mound was left up to me. But once I had the magazine's approval, I dallied around for a while. I went up again to the stadium, sitting this time high over the field in the first row of the third tier where the ushers periodically remind you over your shoulder to keep the paper cups of drinks off the cement balustrade. Far below, Chicago's Early Wynn performed against the Yankees. I watched him carefully. In a few weeks I would be out there myself—I thought uncomfortably—in that perfect circle of the mound around the slab of rubber, in front the raw marks kicked up by the flurry of the pitcher's motion, and then back, almost on the infield grass, the white sock of the rosin bag which Wynn didn't touch that day, being one of the few pitchers who doesn't use it to dust his fingers dry. He calls the pitcher's mound his "office—a place where I conduct my business," and he performed in it with a mean toughness, a pathological hatred of the batter, staring down at him, unshaven, with a baleful glare evident even from the third tier. From up there the malevolence had a physical quality: an attitude of carriage, a heavy sloping walk from the mound when he was done with an inning, moving for the dugout glaring ahead hard as if he was going in there to destroy something in the shadows by the watercooler—a batter, any batter, you felt, they were the enemy, even those on his own team, and you noticed they sat apart from him in the dugout. He is a fair hitter for a pitcher, but when he came up to bat he struck out quickly with cumbersome strokes—like ax strokes—and he stepped away from the plate sloughing his spikes through the grass as if he'd fouled them in the silage of the batter's box. I wondered about that attitude, so noticeable, wondering how long the belligerency blazed, if it was steady, or if after the game in the locker room it faded, and he shaved and felt better about things, perhaps sufficiently to let a batter precede him through the clubhouse door on the way out, and then a pleasant equanimity existing until his next pitching assignment approached, and with it the temper slowly stirring up, rising like a thick yeast.

As I watched him pitch, what began to stir in me that day was not an attitude, but a move of uneasiness which induced cigarettes and under the seat I kept a paper cup of beer, sipping from it and forgetting and putting it up on the balustrade. Down below, the pitcher's circle seemed an alien place, and I looked at it as the apprentice fighter must see the ring the first time he comes up the aisle, seeing it under the harsh lights and the officials leaning on the ropes, waiting. Wynn pitched a four- or five-hitter that day, as I recall, an efficient execution, and I remember observing later that it was a performance that lacked character—simply a passionate yet cold and grim extinction of the batters.

So his performance was methodical; you felt he was impervious to all influences but his own rage. The Yankee bench never tried to rile him; even the big crowd was quiet. On my way home I wondered if such a pitcher could find in his career one moment, one act, that was a monument to the rest, and I doubted it in Wynn's case. In some careers it was easy to spot—the grand gesture that reflected ability and character: Babe Ruth's called-shot home run in Chicago, the slugger pointing into the deep right-field stands, and then hitting a baseball in there and into the derision which expired abruptly in those thousands of throats; or Ted Williams's last home run into the late-autumn gloom of Fenway Park, marking his last at bat with a gesture that served less to punctuate his career, rounding it off neatly, than to show once again his contempt for critics who doubted his artistry. In Wynn's career you felt that there was no such moment—that one victory was indefinable from another, the sum of them merging as an unrelenting continuous vendetta....

It wasn't an attribute I could associate with my own career as a pitcher. In school, I had been a fanatic about pitching, throwing stones at tree trunks when there wasn't anyone to play catch with, but my pitching since those days had started a slow descent into decadence. At college, baseball became associated with beer tankards tilted in the grass—informal games where you forgot the score finally and played with softballs, as big as grapefruits, and as unsatisfactory to hit as pillows. And then eventually the nadir was reached in a game of softball organized in a meadow in France, the last game I played in before appearing in the stadium. I didn't tell the editor about it. Most of the participants had never played baseball before. It had to be explained to them as we went along. We used a brightly colored beach ball which didn't travel far in the thick grass of the meadow—bordered on one side by a canal and behind us the Château of Maillebois. The only beaten-down place in the meadow was for two wicker-cased bottles of the *vin du pays* with glasses propped up around. We had two bats: one a broomstick, the other a fence post so heavy that you felt you had to begin to swing it as soon as the ball left the pitcher's hand. Out in left field was a young countess, playing in bare feet, and separated from her friend in right field—an ash-blond girl in toreador pants—by a male center fielder, so the two girls wouldn't get to chatting with each other. The center fielder was very serious about the game: with every pitch he went forward on his toes to get a jump on the ball in case it was hit out his way. He was the one who had suggested the game at lunch in the château—had explained it gravely and organized everyone.

The countess's husband was pitching and she watched him. Sometimes she would call warmly to him "Ah, Teddy" just to let him know she hadn't gone, and he would turn and see her there in the meadow and behind her a stand of cypress trees.

Early in the game the owner of the château came to bat. He refused to remove a blue boating blazer he was wearing; he disdained advice on the proper batting form, and arranged himself in a crouched stance in which he stood on home plate and faced the pitcher head-on—like a tennis player receiving service. He picked out the first pitch thrown near him and with a convulsive sweep of his bat he smacked a towering hit out to the countess in left field. She gave a little high cry, as faint and forlorn as a curlew's; her mouth remained open as she stared into the sky, and she threw up her arms dramatically, fingers wide, the epitome of Anguish in a Victorian mezzotint, and thus she stood rooted while the ball arched over her head and landed beyond her, rolling briefly for the cypress trees. She turned and ran for it, calling out her husband's name "Teddy! Ted-dy!" and we saw her reach the spot where the ball had dropped, fall down, and rise again with the bright ball in her hand; holding it at arm's length she began to spin as stiffly as a weathercock revolving in a capricious wind—working up speed in her turns until she let go, like a hammer thrower, and we watched the ball sail briefly against the sky, headed away from us, a toss that almost reached the distant barrier of cypress. She ran for it again. It was evident from her lack of direction, however, and from her peculiar throwing motion, her light cotton dress spinning at her knees, that the countess might twirl the ball and then herself out of sight, beyond the grove or into the canal. Before she could reach the ball the second time, the zealous center fielder, who'd been shouting, "Peg it to second, Gabrielle!" and yelling at the second baseman to move out for the "cutoff," beat the countess to the ball, sidestepped her headlong rush, and threw the ball mightily toward the infield.

There the château owner, the gold buttons glinting on his blazer, had watched his hit tower over the countess's head, and then, carrying the bat with him, had charged off through the tall grass, swishing through it with great bounds toward third base, and from there, egged on by a multitude of shouts, he swooped frantically from base to base with all the hysteria of an owl trapped in a pantry—shouting Gallic oaths until the center fielder's toss was retrieved by the second baseman, who approached, knees wobbly from laughter, and tagged him out in the vicinity of the pitcher's position. The center fielder wasn't quite so serious after that. The helter-skelter routes of the play were marked by scores of tiny white butterflies flushed up by those hurried passages through the grass and they hung briefly over the meadow as luminous as fireflies.

Afterward, much later, someone knocked the ball into the canal, where it landed with a *thonk,* bounced a few times, and floated, turning slightly, just out of reach. We coaxed it out finally, lying on our bellies above the water's edge and prodding for it with the longer of the two bats, and I remember myriad little green frogs leaping out from under us as if our weight had squeezed them out of the canal bank. It was the end of the day, and when we walked up through the dusk there were lights burning in one of the château towers. . . .

CHAPTER 3

I hurried home from the stadium after seeing Wynn pitch, promising myself that I would train severely—to resuscitate myself from such decadent pastimes as throwing a beach ball under the towers of Maillebois. But the chances came rarely. A week before my scheduled appearance I threw some twenty or thirty pitches to a friend in a field in Bedford Village, but he was wearing a left-hander's glove with no padding, which caused him to let out an occasional sharp yell when the ball caught his palm cruelly. The yell was involuntary, but disconcerting, and after a while his nephew, aged four, wanted to throw the ball around, and rather gratefully we let him.

In New York City, in my apartment, I was able to do only the mildest form of training. I had a baseball (faintly discolored by the dim signatures of the 1940 St. Louis Cardinal team) which I would hold for a time in my hand, jiggling it, getting the feel of it, and then finally I'd wind up and throw it ten or fifteen feet into an armchair. I also bought a rubber ball to squeeze, to strengthen the pitching wrist—doing all this quite seriously.

Carl Hubbell was a rubber-ball squeezer. Bob Feller, the great Cleveland fastballer who holds the astonishing major league record of twelve one-hit games, along with his three no-hitters, spent much of his time not only gripping baseballs and rubber balls in his room, but also wrenching powerful handsprings, and he'd stand around for minutes at a time tossing eight-pound metal balls up and down in the palm of his pitching hand. You were supposed to keep training, even indoors, even if you just sat quietly in the lobby resting your eyes. In his hotel room, Ted Williams of the Red Sox used to survey and perfect his swing by swishing bats in front of hotel mirrors, and on one occasion, misjudging the arc of his swing badly, he demolished a bed which had in it his roommate at the time, a pitcher called Broadway Charlie Wagner.

I found that I didn't have the self-discipline necessary for such dedicated practice. I couldn't squeeze my rubber ball for more than a few minutes at a time. You squeeze a ball for a while, and you look at what you're doing and you say "What the hell..." and you drop the ball into the back of the bureau drawer. Moreover, I did nothing to get my legs in shape; I continued to smoke, and keep late hours, and break training rules that I never really established. I tried to comfort myself with Satchel Paige's theory about the futility of severe training. "I don't generally like running," said the great pitcher. "I believe in training by rising gently up and down from the bench."

One of the difficulties was that I had to spend much of my time on the phone talking to agents, promoters, and officials — trying to get permission to appear in the exhibition game. I had a short set speech prepared—explaining what I wanted to do—but it didn't sound like much over the phone. If you thought about it—wanting to pitch in Yankee Stadium—it was such a preposterous notion that it was difficult not to sound like a boy who expresses a desire to drive a locomotive. In my case there would be a snort at the other end of the line; sometimes whoever I was talking to would say "Whazzat? Let's go through that again, hey?" and when he heard the speech a second time, he would say "What d'ja want to do *that* for?" before referring you quickly to someone else in the vast hierarchy of officialdom, which meant that the whole process could start again.

The man to whom I was referred quite often was Frank Scott, the players' agent—a powerful figure in the world of professional athletics. He is often described as the October Santa—parlaying World Series heroics into lucrative engagements on the banquet circuit for the outstanding players. He's such a success at making money for athletes off the playing field that almost any day on television you can see his clients selling things, showering, shaving. That year many of his ballplayers were hiding behind sandpaper masks in a razor-blade commercial. Sometimes you can see his players extolling a product vocally—their eyes following the lines on the prompt cards.

He was closely identified with a group promoting the game, and he and I had a number of conversations over the phone—always pleasant, but he was skeptical. Most of the time he wanted to know who was to be held responsible. Suppose I got killed. All sorts of things happened on the pitcher's mound. Did I remember Herb Score and that terrible line drive which nearly blinded him? Or suppose I beaned somebody. Did I want to have a Ray

Chapman on my conscience — the fellow Carl Mays killed with his submarine ball?

Finally, in the heat of the World Series, with the exhibition game only a few days away and my appearance still not guaranteed, I took my problem to Toots Shor — the paterfamilias of sports in New York City. He had his old restaurant then, on 52nd Street, where he presided over the oval trough of his big mahogany bar, padding around it to keep company with his faithful who hold belligerently to his oft-quoted belief that a soft drink is something to be consumed between 3:00 and 3:05 p.m.

He took a moment off to listen to what I wanted to do. Halfway through he interrupted: "Yeh, yeh…Gallico, Paul Gallico did that years ago…Jack Dempsey creamed him."

"That's right," I said.

"You gonna box too?"

I told him I was in the light-heavyweight division and hoped to get in the ring, if briefly, with champion Archie Moore.

"You want some advice?"

"Sure," I said.

"Buy out that diet of Archie's, and *use* it — get yourself down to the flyweight division," Toots said. His blue eyes shut tight and his mouth yawned open like a French clown's as the laughter began to shake him. When he'd quieted down, he said: "You do what I tell you, hear? May be saving your life. *Buy that diet.* Or get real nervous: that's a good way to lose weight."

"Toots, thanks a lot," I said. "But at the moment I'm worrying about baseball. I just can't seem to get started."

I explained how I'd been talking into phones for almost three weeks and I couldn't find anyone to authorize my appearance.

"What you need is *cash,*" he said. "That's all—cash. Get your editor to put up cash."

"What for?" I asked naively.

"You're kidding," he said. "What you got to do is tell Frank Scott you got maybe a thousand dollars for his players to divide up, and they'll be so anxious to have you pitch they'll carry you out to the pitcher's mound in a goddamn *divan.*"

Just then my editor, who ate there often, came hurrying past the bar on his way to lunch in the dining room. He had his head down and was moving swiftly, but Toots Shor noticed him and shouted: "Hey *Sid,* hey SID!" Shor has a very loud voice; some of his cronies refer to him as the Loud Adolescent.

James reeled around and sped in toward us without breaking stride, hurrying quickly to lessen the range of the barragelike voice that had turned every head at the bar.

"God Almighty, Toots, what's the matter?" he asked.

"Kid here needs cash," said Toots, pointing at me. "He wants to throw baseballs up there in the stadium, so that means big money for the kid."

James looked at me.

"It has to do with the project—the baseball game," I explained.

"Oh yes," he asked. "I recall."

"Whassamatter?" continued Toots. "You Henry Luce guys *cheap* over there in Rockefeller Center or something?" He brought down a cuffing affectionate blow on James's shoulder blades with an arm that had once hustled troublemakers out of Leon & Eddie's nightclub.

"Look," said Toots. "Set up a prize. Put up a thousand. The

kid'll pitch and the team that gets the most hits off him will divvy up the thousand..."

James looked off toward the dining room. "Not a bad idea," he said.

"Well, what about it?" Toots insisted.

"Why not?" said James slowly.

"Sure," said Toots expansively. He went into more detail.

I would pitch a half hour or so before the scheduled game, first against the entire batting order of the National League, with the American League in the field, and then, while I puffed out there on the mound, the teams would change sides, and I'd start in pitching against the American League. *Sports Illustrated*'s $1,000 prize would be awarded to whichever team got the most hits. We decided there was no point in the pitchers batting, so that meant I'd face eight batters from each team.

There, in its simplicity, was the final plan. James, looking down at his shoes, agreed to it, and then went slowly in and had his lunch.

"That's a lot of pitching," someone said. "Sixteen men in a row."

"Nah. It's a breeze," said Toots Shor. "Go and phone Frank Scott and see what he says."

So I phoned Scott and told him about the $1,000 prize. He said, "Well, well, well, that's fine, that's fine."

"What about the responsibility?" I asked him. I couldn't resist it.

"What do you mean?" he said.

"Well, suppose someone bops me out there with a line drive.

Or suppose I kill somebody out there with my sneaky submarine ball."

"Listen," he said. "Everything's going to be OK. You keep yourself in shape and I'll see you out there Sunday at the ballpark. We'll work out the details then."

He hung up.

CHAPTER 4

N ot long after, I went down to see the promoters in a small office off Union Square to report to them about the prize. Also I wanted to buy a good ticket for a friend of mine who as statistician and observer would sit in the stands and keep careful notes on my performance. I paid for the ticket, and then I asked if they had any advice for me. A promoter named Julie Issacson swiveled around in his chair and asked me if I'd bought any equipment.

"No," I said. "I haven't done anything about it...thought I'd borrow some...maybe up at the stadium."

"Where'd you get that idea at," he said sharply, "that you can borrow equipment up there? Geez*us*." He stuck a cigar out at me, and said: "Very important, what I tell you. Listen. Ballplayers are superstitious—since I am around them all my life and played ball myself eight years I can tell you they are superstitious something terrible."

"I see," I said.

"Never talk to a ballplayer about his slump, that's the first thing. I mean if you ask him things like 'To what do you attribute the cause of your slump?' something like that, he bops you one for asking that—know what I mean?"

"Sure," I said.

"It's not so good to ask him about the wife and kids, but something real personal like a slump, don't go nagging him about it.

"Then," he said, "the next thing is never—and kid, look *out!*—*touch* anything that belongs to a ballplayer: his equipment, his bat, his glove. You go sticking your hands in a ballplayer's mitt and he breaks your jaw for you, know what I mean? He thinks maybe you'll throw him in a slump. So don't go picking up their mitts or bats. Right, boys?" He turned to the other promoters. There were four of them in the office.

"Right, Julie," they all said.

I promised them I'd bring my own equipment. What Issacson had said was surely so. For example, there was Benny Kauff, of the New York Giants, who was obsessed with the theory that his slumps were caused because his bats were tired, and he rested them—and it was easy to appreciate his rage if you picked up a bat of his, one of those recuperating bats, and swished it around. Or big John "Chief" Meyers, also of the Giants, who was convinced each bat contained exactly one hundred hits—how he'd take it if you swiped that bat and reduced its quota by going up and hitting a single with it. And it wasn't only bats. Any piece of equipment seemed endowed with mystical properties. Wes Ferrell, a pitcher on the Boston Red Sox, once blamed a streak of wildness on a new glove he'd just finished breaking in, and when his manager, Joe Cronin, came out and lifted him, he strode for the dugout shouting at the glove, "It's your fault, *your damn* fault," and with the ripping strength of one possessed he dismembered the glove and dropped it behind him as he ducked into the dugout—done with it, leaving it as sad on the edge of the grass as a discarded shoe.

So when I left Issacson's office I started to outfit myself. I picked up a uniform in a downtown sporting goods shop, and uptown I dropped into a sports shop just off Fifth Avenue and bought a Gil McDougald fielder's glove for $4.50. The store had more expensive models on display (a good mitt costs $15) but I picked out the McDougald because its price seemed properly pegged to the amount of pitching I'd planned to do. It had leather-thong bindings and a pre-oiled pocket. I looked over the bats, hefting them, swinging them easily in the little shop. Even the light 32-ounce bats seemed heavy. I should have bought one. I had a bat at home, I knew, but I didn't realize until I looked at it later that it was a softball model. It had a name. It was called the "Little Bomber."

That afternoon I tried out the glove. It seemed essential to get in at least a couple of hours of practice before the game, so with the glove in the back of the car I drove out to the Palisades with Walter Bingham of the *Sports Illustrated* staff. We thought we'd throw the ball around, and since I'd probably get a chance to bat the next day, take a few turns in the amusement park's batting cage. I'd never been in one of those cages before. Bingham explained it was a wire-enclosed area with a machine at one end which served up pitches at varying speeds.

We drove up the West Side Highway in bright cool football weather. On the playgrounds next to the parkway the Saturday games were going on, the footballs twisting across the worn grass, and over the car radio we listened to the Army football team, two thousand miles away, strain toward the Rice Institute goal line.

When we got within sight of the park we could see the high towering screens of the batting cage, but no sign of activity amid the gaudy clutter of Ferris wheels and rocket rides. We parked the car in an empty lot behind a restaurant and walked across to the only concession that appeared to be open — a miniature golf course. It was tended by a man sitting in a wooden candy-striped booth. As we approached he took out two putters and laid them on the counter. We pointed across at the batting cage. It was the adjacent concession. "Closed?" we asked.

"Whole park's closed," he said. "Everything's been shut down a week or so, everythin' 'cept the golf."

I said we weren't interested in golf but were anxious to hit baseballs. Having come all that way, it suddenly seemed very important to get in the batting cage.

"Take a look," he said. "Everythin's shut down."

"You suppose you could get that thing going for us?" I asked, pointing at the machine in the batting cage.

He gestured at his golf course with its iron-pipe and auto-tire fairways. "I'm the golf man," he said simply.

"Sure," said Bingham. "But perhaps you know someone who has the key... I mean it can't be very hard to operate."

"Look," the man said. "I'm the *golf man*... like I give golf sticks to the people who want to play golf."

We stood for a while. "Well, have you any suggestions?" I asked him. "We're on an assignment," I said. "It isn't as if we wanted to bat baseballs just for the fun of it."

The man reached out and put away the two putters.

"Look," said Bingham. "Is there a batting cage like this one within driving distance, within, say, even ten, maybe fifteen miles?"

"Fifteen *miles!*" The man stared past us at the batting cage. Well, he wasn't sure, but he thought there was a batting cage in an amusement park a long hitch down Route 17. He'd passed it a few times. Bingham and I kept at him. We wanted to know about traffic conditions on Route 17, whether he thought we could pull in there before dark, and if it was dark did the batting cage stay open under floodlights.

He tried manfully to answer us. Suddenly he could see that we weren't trying to josh him — that for reasons I'm quite sure he had no intention of trying to fathom it was essential that we swipe away at baseballs long into that autumn evening. He applied himself diligently — trying so hard to help us that I think in his mind's eye that distant batting cage loomed more distinctly by the second as he talked. "Lights?" he said. "Why they have just *rafts* of lights over that cage..."

We left him finally and set off purposefully for the car. But once in the parking lot we reconsidered. The trip down Route 17 didn't seem worth the bother. So we took off our coats, draped them across a car fender, and started tossing the ball back and forth. The leather lacings on the $4.50 McDougald glove snapped almost immediately, but I tied them together and we continued. The arm felt tired. A family of Chinese watched us from the restaurant window, and when the restaurant door swung open, it momentarily let out the sound of the football fans bellowing over the television. Back toward the amusement park I caught a sudden glimpse of the golf man. He was standing there in the meticulous clutter of his course watching us hurling baseballs grimly through the dusk. He caught me looking at him, and he turned back quickly...for his booth, I suppose, to sit in there with his putters and watch the lunatic facade of the amusement park—shrouded now for the winter, the giant maw of the fun house blocked by a board fence—blur and fade into the evening.

CHAPTER 5

That night the McDougald glove was stolen from my car—taken by someone meandering along looking for the feeble pickings found in unlocked cars and glove compartments and he'd seen the mitt and grabbed it.

That morning I'd come hurrying down a little late, carrying with me a handbag—in it the baseball uniform and a pair of spiked shoes—and when I didn't see the baseball mitt lying in the back of the car where I'd left it, I burrowed around and turned up two crushed road maps, and a scarf, three shotgun shells, a number of soda bottle tops, and a blue plastic duck. I could scarcely believe the glove wasn't among that jetsam of forgotten days. I looked hurriedly up the street. It was deserted. Usually there are stickball games going on, and my first impulse was to buy a glove off a participant's hand. Issacson's warning of the previous afternoon was firmly entrenched in my mind. It seemed unthinkable to arrive at the stadium without a glove.

I ran back up to my apartment and spent fifteen minutes on the phone. In some distant apartment I'd hear it ring, endlessly it always seemed, and when it was answered, usually by a voice nearly muted with sleep, I'd give my name, and then, trying to be unhurried and nonchalant, almost as if it was an afterthought, I'd ask if they happened to have a baseball glove lying around that I could borrow.

"Whazzat? What d'ja say?"

My self-control would vanish.

"Listen," I'd cry into the phone. "Haven't got time to explain, Charlie, but I *gotta* have a fielder's mitt. I'm right-handed. You got one or not?"

I could hear him breathing at the other end of the line.

"And maybe a bat? I got a softball bat here called a 'Little Bomber,' but I don't think I can keep my self-respect up there at the stadium carrying around a bat called the 'Little Bomber.' Do you?"

"Hey, old man," he'd say. "It's nice to hear from you and all — but it's Sunday morning and Priscilla and I did the town last night…"

I would say "Right, right, right," and hang up on him fast and try someone else. Bingham, I thought, my companion of the previous afternoon, but I remembered he was a southpaw. I continued to flip through an address book.

The seventh person I called reported he had a baseball glove in the back of his closet which he hadn't looked at in years. He'd last used it playing third base for Pomfret when he was thirteen, and he was afraid it wasn't in such good shape. That was all right, I said, it didn't make any difference as long as it was a glove.

He lived in a modern apartment house in the East Eighties. A fountain played in the lobby and the automatic elevators had music piped into them. The door to his apartment was ajar. He heard me coming, running hard down the hall from the elevator which sighed shut behind me, and with his face gray with fatigue he stepped out, carrying a half-eaten piece of toast in his hand.

"Sunday morning," he said, "I'm not at my best."

"Where's the glove?" I said.

"I don't know whether you're going to thank me for it," he said. "The glove's really in rough shape. The mice have been at it or something. In fact," he went on, "I was nearly sick when I first saw the ruin of that mitt. Had to get into the back of the closet to get the thing, crawl in there and all..."

"Look," I said. "I haven't any choice. I gotta have that glove. I'm due up there now."

"Yes, Yankee Stadium," he mused. "What the hell is all this about?" He looked up inquiringly. "Maybe I don't want to know, what? Or maybe I'm not awake yet, what? But I'll tell you one thing for sure: that I'd have bet this glove'd never see action up *there,* for chrissake."

Almost angrily he turned back into the kitchen and came back with a flabby black object which he handed me. "Look at that thing," he said. "That's gonna be about as useful to you up there as a dead owl."

I took it and turned it over. "My God," I said.

He shrugged.

"You haven't got a bat, have you, Ed?" I asked. "And I mean something more substantial than a mop handle."

He shook his head. "No bats," he said. "Listen, you going through some sort of comedy routine up there? Something like that? Maybe I'll come up and catch it."

I turned without answering him, mumbling my thanks, and

back in the elevator, the music streaming down, I looked at the glove more closely. The thumb had been ripped or chewed off—quite cleanly, so that there was just a cavity through which my own thumb, when I put my hand in the glove, showed clear down to the joint. I could wiggle my thumb around freely, which I did, staring at it numbly. The lacings had vanished, the bright eyelets empty, and there was a soft patch of mold in the pocket. The glove looked like a seal's flipper. When I reached the car I shoved it into the carryall and tried to forget about it. But Issacson's warning kept nagging. I took a circuitous route up to the Triborough Bridge—tires whining as I whirled through side streets. I still hoped to find a stickball game and a player who'd sell me his glove...a forlorn chance on that cool sun-drenched Sunday morning in late autumn: those who looked up at the squeal of tires were either worshippers on their way to church or perhaps a group headed for the park tossing a football back and forth.

What made me forget about the glove problem, if temporarily, was being delayed at the Triborough Bridge by the arrival of President Eisenhower's motorcade coming into the city from LaGuardia Airport. I leaned out of the car, halted at the end of a long line, and shouted at a policeman: "Hey! Due up at stadium! Can I get through?"

He walked over in that slow, calculated amble of his kind, but his face was bright with interest.

"You playing up at the stadium?"

"Sure," I said. "Due up there now."

"Got the big All-Star game up there."

"That's right," I said.

He was trying very hard to place me. He looked down into the car, smiling, waiting for me to say who I was—Rocky So-and-so, or Whitey So-and-so—waiting for me to give a familiar name to which he could say "Sure, sure," but I kept smiling at him, both of us waiting for the other, until finally he broke first and let me sneak out of the line of waiting cars and into the entrance of the Major Deegan Expressway. In the rearview mirror I could see him looking after me as he walked back to his post. Perhaps by then he'd decided who I was, and when the motorists questioned him he would say, "Why that's So-and-so of the Tigers. Had to get up to the stadium. Sure, that's who. Knew him soon as he drove up."

I was delayed once again. I had come off the expressway fast, down the stadium exit, past the light tweed-colored fortress of the food market, above its battlements the big clock face at which I glanced to see how late I was and found it vacant, the hour and minute hands missing; then I came across the vast parking lot, empty at that early hour, heading for the players' gate, still going fast, and as I pulled up and parked, perhaps a hundred youngsters broke from their positions by the gate, where they'd been waiting to gawk at players on the way in, and they began milling around the car. I had a sports-car convertible at that time, and I suppose the natural assumption, seeing that car speed across the parking lot toward the players' gate, would be that it contained a ballplayer. They packed in tight around the car, pushing in their autograph books, programs, little scraps of paper, stubby pencils, keeping up a steady "Hey, mister, hey, mister," while from the back ranks came an insistent "Who is it? Who's the guy?" the heads bobbing, boys jumping up off their toes to see who was in the car, and then jammed in against the car itself was a youngster just large enough to look in over the side of the door, and he was saying clearly, practically in my ear, "Who *is* you, mister, who *is* you?"

Once, on my way to the theater with my mother, the taxi moving slowly on Broadway, a girl looked in at me and shouted "Frankie!" There was a sudden rush and within seconds the car was immobile in a throng waiting, it turned out, for Frank Sinatra to arrive at a premiere. Those up close, faces flat against the windows, could see there'd been a mistake, but with that first shout such a crush developed, with more people coming from every direction, that the cab began to sway on its wheels. Those in the back of the crowd, who could just barely see in, kept shouting "Who's the dame in there with him?" and pressing in to see...until finally a roar went up behind us somewhere and that packed crowd was drawn off us with astonishing swiftness by the arrival of the real article.

The difficulty at the stadium was that there was no way of convincing the crowd that I wasn't the real article, that I wasn't a ballplayer. I said "No, no, no" a few times, but that was taken to mean that I didn't want to sign autographs. They said: "Ah, come on, mister, be a good guy." When I leaned back and reached for the little carryall with the suit in it, and the spikes, and the dreadful glove, someone said, "Lookit, he's got his 'quipment in there," and a moan of awe went up and I could barely open the car door against the press of them looking to see. Once out of the car I had to struggle to hang on to the carryall. Hands kept snatching at it, four or five boys calling out "Lemme carry your bag, mister," as I stumbled slowly toward the players' gate in a tight thicket of waving autograph books and scraps of paper.

There was a friend of mine, Barclay Cooke, waiting at the gate, who saw me coming and said later that it could have been the slow, triumphant advance of baseball's most popular hero, except that towering above the press of youngsters I wore an expression of bleak astonishment—rather like a camel's.

"Hello, Barclay," I called out to him above the babble of voices. His brother is the sportswriter and commentator Bob Cooke, and he was familiar enough with the baseball world to volunteer to help me through the afternoon.

"Come on," he said. "You're late."

Three of us went through the players' gate: Barclay leading the way, nodding familiarly to the guard; then I went through, followed closely by a small boy clutching at my bag. Others grabbing for it had been sorted out by the guard, complaining at him in querulous cries, high-pitched like seabirds, and only one got through. We both had hold of the bag but I didn't notice him until I heard him say "Thanks, mister"—for getting him through the gate—and I looked down at him. He was wearing a Yankee souvenir cap; furthermore, looped from his wrist, he had a fielder's glove, lovably broken in, dark with oil, and I coveted it.

As a boy I don't remember taking a glove with me to watch a big-league game. Now it seems common practice: the boy gets to the park early, in time for batting practice, which he spends roaming the stands behind either first or third, which are the expensive seats but good hunting grounds for snaring fouls, and he must keep an eye out for ushers who might collar him and check his ticket stub, if he has one, to see if he belongs there.

I opened the negotiations with the glove's owner.

"Listen," I said, bending down and talking to him anxiously.

"I don't suppose you'd lend me that glove of yours, just for the afternoon."

He looked up, startled. "Whazzat?" he asked wildly.

"I left mine home...by mistake," I said.

His manner changed abruptly. He was safely inside the stadium, to start with, and it was apparent that my status was not as official as he'd presumed.

"Not for *fawty dollars* I ain't lending this glove," he said, and then, astounded by the temerity of his remark, which he delivered with shrill violence, he blinked nervously at Barclay Cooke and me as be backed off and disappeared down the ramps.

We watched him go.

"What's the matter?" said Cooke. "You serious?"

I explained my problem.

He said: "I got my son here with me. He's in the stands somewhere; he's got a glove with him, but the trouble is he's a lefty."

I thought of Bingham. The populace seemed choked with southpaws.

"Maybe a left-hander's glove'd be better than what I got," I said. "Take a look at this." I opened the handles of the grip, moving in close to Cooke as if I were showing him contraband. He looked in.

"Gawd Almighty," he said.

We walked slowly toward the visitors locker room. Cooke knew the way. "Listen," he said. "When you get in the locker room, talk to the trainer. Maybe he can dig up a glove for you. Maybe Frank Scott can help you. They'll be in there somewhere."

"They'll think I'm some fool sort of comic with that glove," I said. I couldn't rid my mind of the spectacle I'd present on the mound with that black piece of leather draped from my hand.

"Listen," said Cooke, "If you're going to worry, worry about pitching to Mantle. What are you going to do? Throw him a curve, maybe?"

"God, I don't know," I said. I was feeling low and sorry I'd come.

"Well, good luck," said Cooke. "I'll be rooting for you." He put his hand on my shoulder. "It'll all work out," he said with as much conviction as he could muster.

CHAPTER 6

The locker room was crowded. The place was heavy with cigarette and cigar smoke, but it was bright and antiseptic under fluorescent lights. Down at the end of the room I could see a rubbing table, covered at that time with camera equipment, and beyond it two large coolers for soft drinks and beer. The color of the room was a sharp green, everything that color, except for the flesh tones of a "Miss September" taped to one of the big pillars. At the foot of each pillar were low rectangular boxes, about the dimensions of gardener's frames, filled with sand from which a stumpy forest of cork tips protruded, some oozing smoke, and scattered among them were the chaw wrappers—"Day's Work" or "Favorite" or the bright tinsel gum wrappers. Around the walls of the locker room were the open dressing cubicles—their wooden partitions topped with wire mesh, both wood and wire painted that ubiquitous municipal green. In each cubicle was a wooden shelf, hooks with coat hangers suspended, a seat with a footlocker under it, and then out in front a four-legged stool set on a little rubber mat. Sitting on one of these stools was the first ballplayer I recognized: Richie Ashburn, then playing for the Phillies, already dressed for the game in that club's candy cane uniform except for his spiked shoes, neatly placed by the stool, and he was calmly sitting there turning the pages of *This Week*. Most of the other cubicles were occupied by players in various stages of undress. No one looked at me as I stood there, and finally I sidled over to an empty cubicle and put my bag down on the seat.

I stayed in there briefly, looking out. Most of the players were moving around actively—talking and joking. At the mouth of their cubicles others were sitting motionless on their stools, staring down at their stocking feet or out into the locker room with eyes that seemed glazed. I'd seen that look before, remembering it from years ago when as kids we went with our autograph books and the bubble-gum cards to the midtown hotels where the ball teams stayed. I have a difficult time memorizing faces but the ballplayers who were lobby sitters were easy to spot: large men with these vacant expressions, as I remember them, sitting in armchairs so low that they stared out between their knees at the lobby. Their jaws worked slowly on gum. You never saw them reading, and I used to think that, like Rogers Hornsby, they were so dedicated to the game that they didn't read for fear of straining their eyes unnecessarily. Hornsby, after all, to keep his eyes rested, never went to a film in the twenty years of his major league career. Their faces were devoid of expression, as blank as eggshells, yet peaceful as if a mortician had touched them up. They sat for hours, quietly waiting until the time came for them to leave for the park and the rigors of their profession. Only their jaw muscles worked slightly on the gum like a pulse throb as they stared calmly out at the people moving in the lobby among the potted palms. They never looked up when they signed the autographs. They took the proffered book and the pencil, worked the big writing hand briefly across the page, and you took the book off to a corner of the lobby to gloat over the signature — that tangible evidence that you'd been in the presence of a major league star. The first ballplayer who ever spoke directly to me was John Mize, then the big Cardinal first baseman, later a Giant star who hit 51 home runs in the 1947 season.

He said: "You a ballplayer, son?"

"Yes, sir," I said eagerly. "I play on the St. Bernard's Giants!"

He looked up from his armchair. "What's that? That a new triple-A club?'

"No, sir," I said uncomfortably. "That's my school."

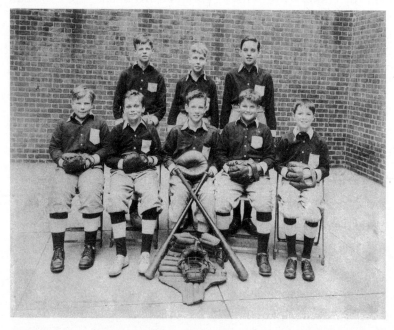

St. Bernard's School baseball team. The author is top left. (*Plimpton Estate*)

He could sense I was embarrassed. "What's your name?" he asked.

"George," I told him.

He put "Good luck to George and the Giants" in the autograph book, and he asked the others with me for their first names to put in their books. When he left the lobby we followed him down the street, at a respectful distance, and when he turned in to a Nedick's hot-dog stand, we stood and peered through the plate-glass window. We watched him drink an orange juice. Then he came out and got in a taxi. We talked about him for days and I almost became a first baseman. His was the prize autograph in the book. He dotted the *i* of Mize with a little circle. I'd never seen an *i* dotted that way and I did it myself for a while until the teachers at St. Bernard's stopped it. . . .

Autographing took up a big portion of a ballplayer's day. To my surprise, even in the locker rooms they were kept at it. Opposite my cubicle was a long table at which sat a group of players writing their names on baseballs in earnest absorption. I went over finally and asked if they could point out Frank Scott. One of them looked up and nodded at a small man at the far end of the room carrying a large manila envelope which he waved heatedly as he talked. "That's Frank over there," the ballplayer said, his pen poised, and then he bent back to his labors. They used ball-point pens, turning the baseballs skillfully as they wrote, and when they were done they put the baseballs in the big red Spalding boxes.

When I went over and introduced myself, Frank Scott looked at me doubtfully. But if our arrangements had skipped his mind, he remembered them when I mentioned the purse *Sports*

Illustrated had offered; he shook his manila envelope vigorously and brightened up. "Yes, yes, yes," he said.

"Is everything arranged?" I asked. "Am I going to pitch?"

"Tell you what," he said. "You just wait around here some-place. When Willie Mays gets here—he's a little late—we'll talk to him. After, we'll go on down and talk it over with Mickey Mantle. They're the captains. They gotta give the final OK."

As he talked, his eyes roved the room, and his sentences were thus delivered with little nods of greeting, small gestures of rec-ognition as he'd glimpse someone he knew. Two men wearing long overcoats came up and gave him the big hello, and I started back to the cubicle. I thought about getting dressed in my base-ball clothes, but when I opened the grip and saw the leather of the glove, I started looking around the locker room for the trainer.

It was at that moment that Willie Mays arrived—the great Giant center fielder, the player Leo Durocher once described in a paroxysm of admiration as "Joe Louis, Jascha Heifetz, Sammy Davis, and Nashua rolled into one." He came into the locker room with a rush, shouting greetings in his high, rather squeaky voice, an arm upraised, waving—smaller, much smaller in stat-ure than I'd imagined, and yet so ebullient the locker room came alive the moment the door swung shut behind him. Suddenly you had to raise your voice to be heard—the room crowded, everyone talking—and in the din it was easy to understand what has been said about Mays: that he would help a club just by rid-ing on the bus with it. His natural enthusiasm was what was infectious—a characteristic one doesn't often associate with the professional. Watching him, you could see that it was almost an unspeakable pleasure for Mays to be where he was: there in the locker room in the blue-green depths of Yankee Stadium, joking with the players, every phrase punctuated with cusswords used not in ill humor but in warmth, in delight, everybody grinning at him as he moved slowly toward his cubicle in the familiar setting of that locker room — the spitboxes, the red Spalding cartons, the uniform waiting on its hook, an afternoon of baseball ahead....

I waited until Mays had completed his tour and then Frank Scott took me over for introductions and to tell him what I wanted to do. Mays listened with his head cocked to one side; when Scott had finished he rolled his tongue in his mouth, considering the matter, and then he looked at me and grinned. "You, man, *you*," he said, "you gonna *pitch?*" and up came a finger, pointing, and then he whistled—one high piercing note—following that with a soft

"Here is Willie Mays. I don't remember what we talked about." (*Garry Winogrand*)

sibilant cussword, drawing it out as an expression of reflection, and then he began to laugh—gusts of laughter so infectious that the knot of people around him began bawling with laughter. It was his way of saying that as far as he was concerned everything was OK because Scott touched me on the sleeve and we left for the Yankee locker room to see Mickey Mantle.

"I mean what did he say?" I asked. "What was all that about? Is it OK?"

"Sure," said Scott as we hurried down the corridors. "Sure."

Compared to Mays, Mantle seemed stolid, almost indifferent as Scott talked to him. During his early years as a Yankee he kept a cap pistol in his locker, and for a couple of seasons around the major league circuit he and Billy Martin used to bang away at each other while Yogi Berra and some of the others would join in with water pistols. But the Mantle I was introduced to by Frank Scott seemed long past the cap-pistol stage. His jaw moved slowly and barely perceptibly on gum. When Scott had finished he gave me one brief flick of his eyes, and he said, "Yeh, yeh." He wanted to know about money, it was apparent, and Scott talked to him earnestly—and very softly as if he were giving him counsel, a hand on his shoulder. I couldn't hear what they were saying finally, so I looked around the clubhouse. It was more spacious than the visiting team's quarters. Even the sandboxes were larger. Being the home club's quarters there was less of the transient and bare atmosphere of the other. Through the door of the manager's office I could glimpse framed caricatures and photographs of Casey Stengel—Stengel, who had said of Mantle in his rookie year, "Well, I tell you this—I got sense enough to play him...."

I looked back at Mantle. He was still listening to Scott,

nodding his head now, affirmatively it seemed—so it looked as though I was really going to get the chance to pitch. While Mantle and Scott continued to whisper I thought perhaps I should find Elston Howard and talk to him. He was scheduled to catch for the American League and thus—though he didn't know it at the time—would be handling my pitches. I'd hoped to see him (and also Stan Lopata, the National League catcher) to discuss signals and try to make up what pitchers call "the book"—that is to say, a reference list of the strengths and weaknesses of the opposing batters. Actually, what distinguishes major league players is that they have no pronounced batting weaknesses. A player wouldn't last who had serious difficulty with a specific pitch. But there are types of pitches a batter prefers, and areas in his strike zone where he'd rather find a pitch. The intention should be, then, to avoid the batter's power, not to think about his weakness but pitch away from his strength. My ability to take advantage of any such knowledge was naturally questionable; but if I was to emulate big-league pitching I felt I should go to the mound with a few tips of this sort. Years back, Crazy Schmidt of the Cincinnati Reds was troubled by a sievelike memory and actually kept his book on his person—in a loose-leaf notebook which he tugged from his hip pocket for reference as each batter approached the plate. "Base on balls" he is supposed to have written opposite the name of Honus Wagner, the great Pittsburgh slugger who won eight National League batting titles.

But I couldn't find Howard, or even recognize him. There were nameplates above cubicles, but they read Rote, Gifford, Conerly, etc.—players on the New York football Giants. Their season was just under way; on a blackboard set against a far wall were the chalked circles and arrows of a football diagram. The only evidence that baseball players were on hand was an inscription someone had written in chalk on a second blackboard. "Mickey Mantle," it read, "and his bloodshot eye nine."

Frank Scott plucked at my sleeve. Mantle had gone back to his stall. "Well, it's all set," he said. "Listen. You're on at one thirty, a half hour before the game's scheduled to start. Both leagues'll send up eight men against you. No need to send up the pitchers. The team that gets the most bases'll divvy up the thousand dollars. They get one point for the single, two for the double, on up to four points for the homers. Right?"

"Sure," I said.

Scott produced a small, chipper smile. "You better get dressed," he said, and he told me he'd see me on the field.

CHAPTER 7

I found my way back to the National League dressing room and sat around for a while until the trainer came by, carrying some towels, wearing a white outfit like an intern's, and I leaned out of the cubicle and said, "Hey!"

He stopped and leaned in. I explained quickly that I was scheduled to pitch in a sort of pregame stunt, but that unhappily I was lacking a glove.

"You're goin' to pitch?" he asked.

"Yes," I said. "But I haven't got a glove. Damn thing was stolen."

"I see," he said dubiously. "No glove."

"As a last resort," I said, "I've got something here."

I let him look in the bag.

"What is that thing?" he asked. "I've never seen nothing like that before."

I said: "If you can't dig me up something, I'll either have to play with that thing, or with a glove somebody's offered which is a lefty's."

The trainer glanced around the dressing room. "Not such a

good idea to borrow a ballplayer's mitt," he said. "They don't like it. Don't like it at all."

"I know that," I said. "I've heard."

He readjusted the towels on his arm. "Well, listen," he said. "I've got a kid who's got a glove. He'll let you borrow it, I reckon, if I can find him."

I said I was very grateful. I told him that if his boy balked, I was quite willing to rent it from him if necessary.

When the trainer had gone, I started to dress. My outfit, from the downtown sporting goods store, was a light-gray jersey and pants, blue-striped stockings, and a baseball cap, the only one which fit properly being a particularly vivid shade of blue— almost cerulean. Since it was the football season, the store hadn't a full line of baseball uniforms. So the jersey hung in folds, but the pants were fine, and the blue cap had a visor which stuck out as long as a swordfisherman's, and when I tried it on and stood in front of the store's mirror I thought the whole outfit looked pretty damn jaunty. But when you pull on that same baseball uniform in a major league clubhouse you don't feel jaunty at all. The sense of being an impostor is strong, and you dress furtively, like a timid bather on a public beach. You think somebody's going to yell at you: "What's up?" Of course, everyone tends to his own business, and I suspect if anyone noticed, he took me for a batboy readying himself for the afternoon—a large batboy, to be sure, since I'm 6 feet 4 inches.

When I was done dressing I looked for the trainer. He was at the far end of the room massaging a player lying on the rubbing table. I went over to see if he'd turned up his son's glove.

On the table was Don Newcombe, the Cincinnati pitcher,

stretched out, colossal, the trainer probing at the muscles of his pitching arm. Under the massage, his muscles rolled and rippled, banks of them, rising from the shoulder blades where a spread of muscle stood out like the *morillo* of a bull, rolling then over the shoulder itself and down the thick length of his arm to fingers which were large and powerful and which with a crackling sound he flexed open and shut hard as if squeezing an imaginary ball. He was grunting with satisfaction as he felt his array of muscles loosen and slack under the trainer's deft fingers. I found the sight intimidating and went back to my cubicle without asking about the glove.

Newcombe and I were born within a year of each other, but as pitchers we have very little else in common. My pitching arm, compared to his, was not much sturdier than a few bones held together by tendons. Casey Stengel once said of a certain skinny pitcher that he threw not with his muscles but with his pulse, and that would have been a fair portrait of my pitching equipment.

As for experience, both Newcombe and I must have started pitching about the same time. I began when I was ten. I wore sneakers in those schoolboy days, had a first baseman's mitt, and at the age of eleven, in the spring, I suddenly learned to throw a lazy roundhouse curveball off the end of a sidearm motion. I don't know what Newcombe's ability was at the age of eleven, but that curve of mine made me something of a phenomenon. The impact on the twelve-year-old that he was going to face a pitch that might slide faintly as it approached the plate gave the pitcher a great psychological advantage. We always crowded around our first batter when he came back to the bench. "Has he got stuff?" we'd ask him, and if the answer was "Yup," we knew we were up against a curveball and we gripped our bats grimly.

Because of that early curveball and the insidious pleasure it gave as it bent past opposing bats, I became interested in variety and trick pitches. Learning from the Spalding manual *How to Pitch,* I started throwing in practice what were supposed to be palmballs, forkballs, and knuckleballs to catchers who would leap for them vainly and call out "Hey, geez, cut it *out*" before turning to stomp gloomily across the long lawns to search for the pitch in distant bushes. Carl Hubbell with his screwball was a particular hero. I'd read somewhere that the effect of his screwball, delivered with a violent inward snap of the wrist, put such a strain over the years on his arm that when he stood relaxed, with his arms down at his sides, the palm of his pitching hand faced out. When I stood around at the age of eleven, having read this, I did the same—faced the palm out, hoping that it would be associated with screwball pitching, and not with a malformation of the arm, which is what it looked like. One day my father finally said: "What's wrong with your arm, son? You fall out of a window?"

"Well, that's from screwball pitching," I said.

I had hoped someone would ask.

Of all the various experiments—the screwballs, the forkballs, and the rest of them—I only kept in my repertoire a curious wild knuckleball which shuddered convincingly, I was told, when it was near enough the plate for the catcher to make a pronouncement about it.

Also, I had a change of pace, which Sal Maglie purports to be the most important pitch in any given repertoire. My version of the pitch, which big leaguers throw pretty much off their regular motion, consisted of a big windmilling windup—grotesquely exaggerated to fake the batter into thinking the pitch was going to be smoked in — then at the last second letting up on the motion to take the speed off the pitch, like trying to make a fellow flinch without hitting him, and the pitch as I threw it, a soft, inaccurate lob, wouldn't have fooled your sister. I rarely threw it. But it was in the repertoire — like a useless but interesting instrument kept in a toolbox in case it should ever come in handy.

Finally, of course, I had a fastball. Joe DiMaggio once wrote that all pitchers are born pitchers, reasoning that there never has been one who didn't have a good fastball — a natural gift which no amount of practice will develop. I practiced anyway, throwing stones if the long-suffering catchers weren't available. The fastball was sufficient, I guess. It didn't hop or anything, or tail off, but it was accurate even if it didn't ever have too much steam behind it. After all, control was the great virtue in pitching and among those early heroes were the control pitchers; I read about them avidly: the legendary Cy Young, who walked a man on an average of one every seven innings, and the great Satchel Paige, who as a stunt could throw strikes over a gum wrapper. Control, if you believed in it enough, was a fine compensation for lack of speed.

But there was no way, sitting in that cubicle, to pretend that my paltry array of pitches was sufficient for an afternoon's work in Yankee Stadium. The last time I'd used them had been years before. It was Newcombe's presence which pointed up the disparity. From where I sat I could still see those long fingers flexing — fingers which could flick a baseball into the strike zone in an estimated three-fifths of a second, which could snap the ball into the sharp twists of the curve, and the slider — these pitches sailing down at you from a high-kicked motion which put his spiked shoe, dripping dust, practically in your face so they said you had to look around it to see what was coming at you... all of that ability and experience coupled with a competitive nature, a long pugnacious jaw, and a bellicose frame of mind to go with it (he would be remembered for temporizing one loss by slugging a parking-lot attendant) — the components, in short, adding up not only to the portrait of a major league pitcher but sufficiently intimidating so that for the first time that day I felt the deep heavy sock of nerves hitting hard in the stomach.

I stared miserably out into the locker room. Actually, the room was crowded and noisy and there was nothing really in that atmosphere to inspire an attack of nerves: across the way Ashburn was getting on toward the end of *This Week;* a few players were still seated around their table pushing ballpoint pens slowly across the horsehide surface of baseballs; the noise and laughter came from tight circles of reporters and admirers surrounding a player, pumping him, and the smoke lifted out thickly, illuminated periodically by the blue blink of a flash camera. No one was aware of me, or questioning my presence in a player's cubicle, and yet my knees were quivering and I began to yawn helplessly — the thick weight of nerves draining me of energy.

Some athletes are absolutely impervious to pregame nerves. Lawrence Waterbury, the 10-goal polo player, would sleep for one hour before the great international matches of his time, lying on his back on a sofa, and when he'd jog onto the field on his polo pony he was yawning away sleep, not nerves. Boston's great athlete Charlie Devens, who had a brief stint with the Yankees as a pitcher, not only took catnaps before a game but occasionally dozed off on the bench during one. His teammates, especially his manager, Joe McCarthy, often took umbrage—McCarthy on one occasion to the extent of jarring Devens awake and shouting at him: "Where the hell ya think y'are? In a canoe?" It didn't make me feel better to know that Devens and Waterbury are exceptions—that almost all athletes, regardless of their ability, suffer jitters before a game. Sometimes they can hide them—like the lobby sitters. Often they can't. Later that year I was to see a great professional, Bob Pettit, the high scorer of the St. Louis Hawks basketball team, beset by a curious manifestation of pre-game nerves. I saw him at a small cocktail party two or three hours before his game was scheduled to start in the Garden, but the game was obviously on his mind. In such a big man (he's 6 feet 9 inches) the small pangs of worry seem magnified, so you wondered watching him if he wasn't *stricken* with grief—his large face melancholy, his manner withdrawn, as with his fingers he busily worked at a paper napkin, ripping out small chunks, rolling them rapidly between his fingers into little balls, and these he would flick at a target—an empty glass, a wastebasket, an ashtray, a bottle cap, and once I got in the way of some target and was hit high on the cheekbone, and turning I looked up into a face so preoccupied that I doubt he knew what he was doing as he moved gloomily through the crowded room trailing after him scores of little paper pellets.

"Hey, kid!"

I looked up startled. The trainer was standing in front of the cubicle, holding out a fielder's mitt.

"Here's m'boy's glove," he said. "Now for chrissake take care of it. If he don't get it back, it'll be hell for both of us."

Just the sight of that glove quieted the nerves. "I won't take my hand out of it," I said, reaching for it gratefully. I slid it on, and tapped my right fist into the pocket. It was brand-new. I told the trainer it was the best-looking glove I'd ever seen, and when he'd left, I sat there gloating over it. In the curious fashion of baseball gloves it had a lot of literature stamped into the leather — namely, the trade name (I think it was called a FieldRite), then the name of the sponsoring player, the patent notice, the strange phrases "autograph registered" and "snap action," and a few other items including the instructive word "pocket" so that you knew where the pocket of the glove was, and impulsively, because I was so pleased after all that morning's worry to have one, I took the glove up to a player wearing the uniform of the San Francisco Giants, and I showed it to him and I said, "Read any good gloves lately?"

I said very little during that long day in the stadium, but I wish I could take back that quip. The player looked at me. "Do I know you from someplace?" he asked finally, not unkindly, and I said no and went back to my cubicle.

CHAPTER 8

A little later, the players started to leave the locker room.
Many of them, just before they'd reach the door, would
shuck the wrapping off a chaw or a piece of gum and you'd see
the jaw begin to chomp down hard. Gum and chaws were a large
part of what was to be remembered about that day: you saw the
wrappers, in the spitboxes or on the dugout floor, and the players'
cheeks puffed out with chaws, the constant spitting, and then
always the jaws working, so that in the dugout you'd often
hear—as a sort of tree-frog background—the slight clicking
and popping of new sticks of gum being broken down. I have
never liked gum, or tried a chaw. One major league player—
Enos Slaughter—chews *both* of them, mixing bubble gum in
with his chaw "to keep it cudded." The chewing, all those jaws
working on something, made a deep impression. Later on, for
example, I heard that Eddie Collins, the greatest of the second
basemen, would remove his gum when he had two strikes on him
and stick it up on the button of his cap. Perhaps he did it to
change his luck, but my feeling is that he must have done it as a
form of chastisement—denying himself the pleasure of that

gum until he got his hit (he was the best two-strike hitter, they say, of all time) — so he could pop that gum back in quickly and gratefully. Deprive a ballplayer of his gum, or his chaw, and he's more uncomfortable than if you threw a hat on his bed — which they spoke of as being the most devastating bit of bad luck that could be suffered.

I kept dawdling around in the locker room. It was time to leave for the field, but I stuck to my cubicle, sitting in there alone, not necessarily enjoying its privacy, but not especially eager to get going. Carefully, I took off one of my spiked shoes, rearranged the sock, pulling it tight around my heel, then settled the foot back into the shoe, doing all this slowly, painstakingly, until finally when I looked up the big locker room was almost deserted. The trainer was fussing in the cubicles across the way; I could hear a shower dripping, and among the locker-room pillars the cigar smoke had settled in a heavy fog bank, fed by thin streams from the sandboxes.

Once outside the locker room, I wasn't sure which way to turn. I wandered briefly in the long corridors. They were crowded: ushers, attendants, vendors. The inch or so the spikes added to my height threw my stride off, and I stalked through the press uneasily, spikes crashing against the cement. At one juncture I looked through an open door into a room crowded with men climbing into ushers' clothes. Before I could move on, one of them looked up. "Hey, man, lookin' for the field?" he asked. He began his grin. He meant it as a joke, of course, taking it for granted that any man in a baseball uniform would know; but then I said, "Yes, I *am* looking for the field," and his grin vanished as if I'd hit him. "Nat'l Leaguer," I explained. "Stranger in this here park." Slowly he came to the door and then he gave me the directions to the National League dugout. They were painfully simple ("Just down there to the left") and I nodded. Behind him I could see the other ushers looking—caught cataleptic, a coat half on, a leg poised over trousers, a hand at a cap's brim....

"Much obleeged," I said. My voice, striving for confidence, took on the nasal whine of the hillbilly; the usage was one foreign to me, one I haven't used before or since, but I said it, "Much obleeged," then turned and hurried for the corridor indicated. It slanted steeply downward to a patch of daylight at the far end; I passed a canvas stretcher hung on pegs set in the wall, and then at the end of the slope I took the few steps up into the bright sunlight flooding the dugout.

In front of me, suddenly, at eye level, was the playing field, unbelievably vast, startlingly green after the dark of the tunnel. In the looming stands the stark symmetry of empty seats was disturbed only here and there by an early spectator. After the reverberating confines of the corridors, the great arena seemed quiet and hollow, and you felt you'd have to talk very distinctly to be heard. But there were new sounds, faint but crisp, the sounds of batting practice, the slap of the ball into the glove, the cheerful whistles of the ballplayers, and these were engulfed in the cavernous spaces under the jade-colored facades, and made echoes of, and while I stood there the incongruous strains of a Hawaiian hula-hula started up over the public-address system and drifted thinly, shredded by wind eddies, through the stands and across the green baize of the playing field.

I sat in the dugout for a while, almost imprisoned by my awe of the scene in front of me. After a while, I was surprised to note, as I sat there, that the dugout is one of the worst vantage points in a ballpark; from his position in the sunken dugout, slouched on the bench, his back to the cement wall, the ballplayer, literally at ground level, has a worm's-eye view of the proceedings on the field. Since the pitcher's mound is raised over a foot above the infield, and the whole field is sloped for drainage purposes, the players on the far side of the pitcher's mound seem to be wading around in a sea of green. As seen from the third-base dugout, the second baseman seems to be in up to his knees, and beyond him the right fielder is in up to his neck, just his face and cap visible above the configuration of the pitcher's mound. I could understand why Casey Stengel complained he couldn't see Albie Pearson, the diminutive American League outfielder, from the Yankee dugout. Literally, if he could see anything, it would be the peak of Pearson's cap. Furthermore, as I sat in the dugout watching, I felt no sense of *perspective*, so that a ball batted out toward shortstop Billy Martin, say, to my untutored eye could have been going anywhere in the infield. Of course, years of watching from the dugout give depth to the flat perspective: "Oh-oh," the ballplayers would say. "Billy's goin' t'have trouble with that one," and sure enough, the ball would just skip by him into the outfield.

During this time the dugout was deserted, the ballplayers out on the field. Like the cubicle back in the locker room, it was safe—a *querencia*—and I slouched down on the bench. On the wall at one end was a printed notice which read "Players Must Not Bat the Ball Toward the Grandstand During Practice." I read the sign, and then reached out and picked up a protective plastic helmet from a pile on the dugout steps. I tried it on over my blue cap. It tipped down over one ear and I heard the faint crowd noise, the hula-hula music, the chatter of players on the field, amplify and murmur like the sea sounds of a conch. I straightened the helmet. I stood up and ran a hand over the handles of the bats set in their racks. Then I went down the length of the dugout, down the duckboards chewed raw by spikes, to inspect the watercooler. The watercooler is traditionally the target of attacks by outraged ballplayers, usually a kick or a blow with the palm of the hand. The one I was inspecting seemed to have escaped undue damage; a push at the plunger produced a prompt stream of water; it worked with a faint and disdainful electric hum. I was peering down its sides when I looked over my shoulder and saw that Don Newcombe had come into the dugout. He was settling down on the bench, his great jaw working on some substance. He was watching me. I put on my glove, tapped my fist into it, and hurried up the three steps onto the playing field.

They say that the first time Lou Gehrig was called upon to bat in the major leagues he ran up those same three steps (the Yankee dugout used to be on the third-base side), slipped and fell headlong among the bats (which in his day were laid out in rows in front of the dugout), and then, crimson-faced, everybody guffawing behind him, went on to the plate to strike out on three pitches. I don't mean to suggest that my first steps on the playing surface of Yankee Stadium were as embarrassing; but for me, at least, they are just as painful to recall. A few steps away from the dugout, conscious that Newcombe was watching me, I realized I was still wearing the batter's plastic helmet. I reached up for it, but it tumbled loose from my grip. It fell and rolled in the dust. I bent quickly to pick it up, clawing at its tortoise-smooth sides, but just as I got a grip on it, my blue cloth cap fell off. Holding the helmet in my free hand, I tried to pinch up the cap with the leather fingers of the fielder's mitt, but succeeded only in shoving the cap along the ground, hunching along after it like a hunter after a crippled partridge.

All this was played out in front of the dugout—as if Newcombe was sitting in the orchestra pit looking up at a stage on which a performer was indulging in some grotesque pantomime of awkwardness.

By the time I'd managed to scoop up the cap I surely could have made a joke of the whole thing, and then sat down in the dugout with Newcombe and asked him for bits of pitching lore. Perhaps he could have helped me prepare my "book" on the hitters. But, as it was, when I stepped into the dugout, holding both cap and helmet, I looked miserably into his long-boned face, laid the plastic helmet down among its fellows, and jumped back out for the playing field. I had spooned up so much dirt in my cap as I'd pushed it along the ground that when I slapped it back on my head, the red dirt poured past my ears in a cascade and pattered around my feet. I don't know what Newcombe made of it all. There was a lot of dirt in that cap. He must have noticed it.

CHAPTER 9

O ut on the field there was enough going on to keep you active, to keep your mind off the embarrassments of the past and the commitments of the future. In front of the dugouts, some of the players were still warming up, tossing the ball back and forth; a few pepper games were in action—a batter chopping short grounders to three or four of his teammates—a number of these little games going on so that all around, along with the slap of the ball into leather, you heard the clean sharp sound of the ball against the hard ash of the bat. Another sound you heard, above the steady and increasing hum of people moving into the stands, came from the long thin fungo bats that give off a sound as if they were made of cork when they loft out the high practice flies to the outfield; you could watch the ball hang out there forever above the rim of the stadium, hit so high that when the fall started, it was absolutely perpendicular into the glove of the distant fielder, who moved under it gracefully, jogging a few steps after catching it, and then lobbed it stiffly, as if his arm was sore, in to a relay man out behind second base; he would pick it up and roll it in toward the fungo hitter, where it would lie for a while before perhaps being picked up, given a little toss, and then with the slight pop of the fungo sent out again on that long climb above the stadium rim. There was no lazier or more pleasant pastime than watching good fungoes hit, unless it was catching them. I wanted to run to the deep outfield and try, particularly in the infamous left field of Yankee Stadium, supposedly the most difficult field in the major leagues, where often you see a fielder stumbling around as if fighting off a wasp—a nightmare sun field where apparently the sun and the cigarette haze combine to remove the perspective from a fly ball's flight.

But it was more important to get the pitching arm limbered up, so I resisted going to the outfield and looked around for someone to warm up with. I hoped to sidle up to a pair tossing the ball back and forth, and find that easily and without any explanation necessary I'd be included. But such wasn't the case. I'd stand in alongside Gil Hodges, for example, tossing the ball with Stan Lopata. Tapping my glove speculatively, I'd wait for Lopata to throw me the ball. But he wouldn't. He'd throw it to Hodges, and Hodges'd throw it back to him, and he'd throw it to Hodges, and I'd watch the ball hungrily, and if I had sufficient brass and self-assertion I would have called down to Lopata, "Hey, *Stan*-baby, watcha think I'm standing heah for...for the love o' Mike throw me the *ball!*"

But I didn't yell anything like that. I moved off quietly to another pair, and being frustrated there, went on to another, and finally I ended up warming with the National League batboy.

He was about fourteen or fifteen, I'd guess, a stocky fellow wearing a Cincinnati cap which Don Newcombe had given him.

He was proud of it. He said Newcombe was "terrific." He called him "Newk" and he referred to the other players by their first names and with easy familiarity. "Junior—that's Jim Gilliam of the Dodgers y'know—" he would begin, "was saying just a while ago..." and then he would chatter on about what Gilliam had said, his information peppered with ballplayers' nicknames and statistics such as the weight of so-and-so's bat. He had an open friendliness that kept him talking while we tossed the ball back and forth and occasionally I would say, "Is that so?"

After a while he said he had to quit because he had his job to do. At the time I envied his poise, that confident rather shrill voice gossiping on, and particularly that he had work to keep him occupied. I don't mean to suggest that I was intimidated by everyone in Yankee Stadium that day, but if one is to be accurate about these things, you did envy those who had clear-cut jobs to do—even if it was looking after bats, or selling hot dogs, or ripping tickets in half at the gate. You envied the people coming into the stands who would sit in the sun, and the ushers who looked at their ticket stubs and used a dusting mitten on the slatted seats and got a quarter for doing so. At least, their immediate future was predictable; the worst that could happen to the majority of the people would be a little mustard spilled on the shirt front or perhaps the team of their choice would lose.

But for me the future was uncertain and perhaps the best I could hope for was survival without shame. From time to time I'd look out at the pitcher's mound and then beyond at the Longines clock in the scoreboard out past deep center field. I'd say to myself, "Bo, in one hour (or half an hour, or twelve minutes—whatever it was) you're goin' to be out there, you damn-fool aggressive *nut!*" and the punch of nerves would come, deep in the stomach, just about bending me over.

And yet you knew that if someone leaned over the box railings and offered to change places you'd ignore him. Simple curiosity kept you going; and also a sense of resignation — as if it had all been set inexorably in motion long ago, that day when Mantle hit his home run and the idea crossed your mind to try the big leagues for an afternoon.

And then from time to time, even in those attacks of nerves, there was exhilaration — in which you suddenly looked at everything through the pop eyes of the rookie just coming up, seeing Yankee Stadium for the first time, and touched by his same foolish excitement. Temporarily, you forgot your inadequacies and the stigma of being an impostor. The single fact that you had on a uniform and wore a glove made you a ballplayer. There were odd moments — and they came increasingly as the afternoon went on — when you felt not only comfortable but confident. Once, I heard someone shout, *"Hey, kid!"* and I went over to a box near the Yankee dugout and there was Toots Shor. He had a big grin on his large, pleasant face, and when I got to the box railing he threw a big affectionate jab and said, as I recall, "How's the soupbone?" — asking after the condition of my arm — and so I leaned against the railing and told him. I told him it was a little rusty, but then I found myself talking in a low confident drawl about that arm as if it was a property of great distinction and value. It didn't make any difference, or at least not too much difference, that you heard someone down the line saying, "Who's that gabbing with Toots? The batboy? Great big batboy, eh?" and you heard the other one say "You got me,

Charlie, but he ain't no batboy. Toots Shor talking to a batboy? You nuts?"

When my warm-up associate had bustled officiously off on his labors, proud under his Cincinnati cap, I wandered around the field for a while. There were many men in mufti on the playing field—photographers, officials (occasionally I'd see Frank Scott and nod at him), reporters, and here and there you'd see the motion-picture cameras set up on tripods, the lens aimed at a ballplayer and his interviewer—the latter cheerful and eager, asking his questions through a quick nervous smile, rarely looking at the ballplayer beside him. You'd hear him ask: "Well, how d'ja think the season went for you, Bob?" and then he'd shift the thin rodlike microphone to the ballplayer, who was usually tall and ill at ease, and he'd glower down at the microphone and say, "OK, I guess." Then the interviewer would snatch the microphone back and say into it, cheerfully yet earnestly, "Well, d'ja think you'll do better next season? Or what?"

Sometimes, of course, a player would display confidence in front of the microphone that bordered on the brassy, and the air around would boom with a ruckus of pleasantry and affection. "Well, Harry, it was just great t'talk to ya, and thanks a mile f'having me on the show," the ballplayer would say, leaning forward after the microphone like a horse after a stalk of grass as the interviewer sought to snatch it back, so that with their heads close together their esteem babbled into the microphone from two fronts at the same time. Eventually the ballplayer would leave, and the interviewer would shake his head slowly, a look of reflection, even of awe, on his face to indicate that we'd all been in the presence of someone pretty special.

I hung on the fringes of these interviews, listening, and then I'd move on. No one took any notice of me except on one occasion when a photographer, crouched behind a boxlike still camera set on a tripod, told me I was in the way. I stepped quickly off to one side and watched. His subject was a ballplayer I didn't recognize. Briskly chewing his gum, he was standing waiting for the photographer's instructions.

"OK," the photographer said finally. "Make like you're fielding a grounder."

The ballplayer stopped chewing. He dropped quickly into a crouch, grotesquely stiff, as if he was being clubbed to the ground; he placed his glove down by his shoe tops, and across his face a look by which he meant to indicate intense determination — as if a baseball was actually skipping toward him. In truth, with his eyes staring, he seemed to wear a look of horror — as if what he was going to field was not a baseball but the onrushing charge of a large and wildly berserk animal.

"OK. *Great!*" said the photographer.

The player straightened up, his face suddenly bland and peaceful, and the jaw began to work again on the gum.

CHAPTER 10

———

A fter a while, I insinuated myself into a pepper game going on behind home plate. Backed up against the stands were Bob Friend, the Pittsburgh pitcher, and Richie Ashburn and Frank Robinson, both outfielders. The three of them stood abreast, fielding the grounders and lobbing the ball out about forty feet to Ernie Banks, the Chicago shortstop, who would flop his bat out loosely and chop the ball back to each of them in turn. I went and stood next to Friend, wondering if their pepper game was as exclusive as the warm-up had been earlier. But as soon as I set myself, Banks sent a grounder skidding across the grass at me. It popped cleanly into my glove, and I straightened and tossed the ball back for him to chop toward Robinson at the far end of the line.

Friend, next to me, glanced over. He'd had a fine year with the Pirates, winning twenty-two games, and he was one of the players I was looking forward to talking to. He said: "Well, how are you comin' along? Enjoying yourself?"

"It's all a little new," I said. "I don't feel at home, or anything like that."

"Well, I'll tell you something," Friend said. He stopped and fielded a grounder. "This is my first time in this park—being in the other league and all—and I don't feel all that much at home either."

It was a comforting thing to hear. I was put at ease, and I found I could truly enjoy the pepper game. But as soon as I was put at ease, and felt at home, I found it almost impossible to talk to Friend. I began to envelop myself in the fiction of actually being a ballplayer. I knew that with the first question I asked, I would be marked for what I really was: an observer, a writer, an outsider. So I stubbornly refused to betray the image of myself as a ballplayer by asking questions, and I began to strengthen the fiction as the afternoon progressed by adopting a number of curious mannerisms I associated with ballplaying: my voice took on a vague, tough timbre—somewhat Southern cracker in tone—and the few sentences I spoke were cryptic yet muffled; I created a strange, sloping, farmer's walk; once I found myself leaning forward on my knee, spiked shoe up on the batting-cage wheel, chin cupped in hand, squinting darkly toward center field like a brooding manager; I was sorely tempted to try a stick of gum, despite my dislike of the stuff, in order to get the jaws moving professionally. Sometimes I just moved the jaws anyway, chewing on the corner of the tongue.

The trouble with the role was that my responsibilities as a writer were eclipsed. I never wrote down any notes. I rarely asked questions. There was Friend, a foot or so away, and yet I could ask none of the questions I had planned to put to him. After our first exchange of pleasantries we remained silent. He would have been interesting to talk to. He is an affable and intelligent citizen, I had been told, the player representative of the Pirates, a Purdue graduate, and a student both of the piano and the investment business which he works in during the off-season. He has a round, pleasant face, unnaturally pale compared to the cowboy-rough appearance of most ballplayers, but with a serious mien you wouldn't be surprised to find behind a rolltop desk at One Wall Street. Yet he is easygoing enough to have a reputation of top prankster on his club, being considered an artist among his teammates in the practice of "lighting shoelaces," which I suppose is a variety of hotfoot. It would have been particularly interesting to hear Friend talk about nerves. When he first came up to the major leagues the tension bothered him and he fidgeted through his pitching assignments with his face drawn haggard, his fingers twitching at his cap, at the rosin bag, and he peered bleakly at his teammates from the confines of the pitcher's mound as if he'd been imprisoned in a cage. His teammates tagged him with a Runyonesque nickname. Nervous Nervous, they called him, Nervous Nervous Friend.

But of course I didn't ask him about that or any of the other things. I continued chewing on the corner of my tongue and concentrated on the pepper game. At one point I was tempted to tell him what the batboy told me Junior Gilliam of the Dodgers had said, the only small talk I had to offer, but I didn't. So we stood mutely in the pleasant sun, occasionally bending for the grounders that would skip across the grass from Banks's bat.

I wasn't the only one who had a problem in communication. Just behind us, his face pressed against the wire screen, was a youngster with his fielder's mitt and also an autograph book. He'd started at the far end of our quartet. "Hey, Robinson," you could hear him piping. "Hey, sign, hey, Frank."

Ballplayers rarely stop their pregame schedule to sign autographs, but he was persistent. Down the line he came. "Hey, Richie, hey, Richie Ashburn," he said, but everyone remained aloof, silent, moodily intent on the pepper game. When he came to Friend, next to me, he said, "Hey, Friend, come on, Bobby," with no luck, of course, and then it was my turn. He paused for a long time. You could hear him puzzling, the crisp sound of his scorecard being inspected for a clue as to my identity, and finally, the wire screen creaking as he leaned against it, he said slowly, "Hey, *mister*."

I heard Friend chuckle.

"Hey, mister!" the youngster repeated. He rattled the pages of his autograph book, but I took my cue from the others and didn't budge. I felt a kinship with him, though—both of us outsiders peering in, ignored, in limbo—but I continued to stare stolidly out at Banks.

That was the only time that day on the playing field that I wasn't referred to as "kid." As a spectator in the stands they call me "chief," as in "Hey, *chief*, pass the peanuts down to the guy in the hat." But on the playing field it was "kid." I never heard anyone else called "kid," except for the players whose first names were Billy—Martin, and Pierce of the Chicago White Sox. It was a term reserved, apparently, for the outsiders, or the newcomers—and, knowing that, it was galling to hear. The ballplayers called each other "boy" or "baby"—often tacking the appellative to the given name as in "Jimmie-baby" or "Gil-boy." "Baby" was the most affectionate usage, either drawn out long, *bay-bee,* or pronounced short, so that it sounded French, as if you were enunciating the initials of Brigitte Bardot. That was the way you usually heard it: *"How t'go, bé-bé."* The *baby* is ubiquitous. In Italy, in the leagues starting up there, the holler-cry from the shortstops is *Va bene, baby, va bene.* But for me that day it was always "kid."

When the pepper game broke up (it seemed to break up without anyone saying anything, automatically, as if instinctively the ballplayers knew when to move on to the next phase of the pregame schedule), I wandered idly over to the batting cage. Harvey Kuenn, then playing for the Tigers, was batting—striding forward from a stance deep in the batter's box that reminded you of the photos of Rogers Hornsby, the rear foot pulled away from the plate, and he lined the pitches out sharply. It was about Kuenn that Casey Stengel once said: "If the guy was hurt, his team might be hurt, but the pitching all over the league will improve." When he'd finished his batting he came over and stood nearby. I looked at him and he said, "They tell me you're goin' to pitch."

"That's right," I said. "Just enough to see what it's all about."

He leaned on his bat, and after a while he said: "You want to hit?"

"Sure," I said. "Damn right."

"Wait'll the guy gets out of there," he said, nodding at the cage, "then you go on in."

He handed me his bat. "Remember," he said. "Keep the trademark—the label there—facing up."

"Sure," I said—with a twinge of disappointment that he'd thought me so unknowledgeable as not to know this first principle of batting. I hoped no one standing around had overheard.

In the batting cage was Rocky Colavito. Deep in right you could hear the youngsters waiting with their gloves calling at him to pull one in the stands out there, and then you'd hear him grunt as he applied his power to try to satisfy them. He hit some majestic drives, the ball going away from you fast, suddenly as limber and small as a golf ball against the distant clifflike stands, and you weren't quite so eager to bat seeing the distances he could reach. After each drive, Colavito arches his back, as if an insect was bothering him between the shoulder blades, and then he readjusts his feet in his wide stance, points his bat at the pitcher, and he's ready. He's a handsome player, the idol then of Cleveland, now of Detroit, with dark slack good looks and the pouting mouth of a rock-and-roll singer. When he finally finished batting he stepped out of the cage and removed his cap, perhaps to mop the sweat from his brow, perhaps to display his hair which is as composed and sleek as a bullfighter's.

Harvey Kuenn said: "OK, kid...go ahead in there. Keep the trademark facin' up."

I ran into the cage, settling myself quickly in the batter's box, not wanting to waste anybody's time being finicky and I swung at everything the batting-practice pitcher threw. He was Ralph Houk, the Yankee coach, pitching from behind a protective canvas screen, belt high, which he ducks behind at the end of his delivery — not with me up there but when he's throwing to someone like Mickey Mantle. His job is just to lay the pitches across the plate and I swung viciously at them, hitting two ground balls, high slow hoppers, one down the third-base line, the other down toward first, feeling the bat sting my hands, and then one hard low line drive which bounced just in front of first base and rolled down the line into the right-field corner. It would have gone for a single, I prefer to think, unless the first baseman was playing on the bag. Frankly, I think about that hit occasionally, perhaps too much, since anyone able to heft a bat could have hit those batting-practice tosses. But the circumstances and the surroundings were such that you remember: the ball coming in and stepping forward to lash at it and the clean feel of the solid hit and even if the ball didn't get out of the infield on the fly you had such a sense of accomplishment that you felt like installing yourself in the batting cage until forcibly removed. Reflections of this sort had to come later, because at the time Ralph Houk picked up another ball and threw down a pitch which I swung at mightily—trying to drive it into the outfield—and missed. The ball smacked into the canvas at the back of the cage, and as I swung around, almost falling down in the batter's box, I saw Mantle and Bob Cerv leaning on their bats, looking on, waiting, and so I hopped out of there.

I was excited. I hurried over to Kuenn. "Damn," I said. "That's damn good fun."

He shifted his chaw slightly. He said "spray hitter"—meaning the hits had gone to all fields—saying it reflectively and not as a compliment but as a professional appraisal. One had the strange feeling that he filed his evaluation away in some compartment of his mind...that if in the obscure chance I should turn up on an opposing team in the far future he would scratch around and remember and then shift in his defensive position accordingly.

I stood and watched the batting practice only briefly. The distant clock indicated less than fifteen minutes before my scheduled start. I looked hastily for someone to start warming up with. A player wearing a catcher's mitt was ambling slowly down the line from third base. The mitt was what caught my eye...there wasn't time to hunt up a scorecard and check to see who he was. I hurried over to a trio of reporters standing by the batting cage — deep in agitated colloquy. I apologized to them for interrupting, and I pointed to the approaching player and said, "Who's that?"

The reporters were puzzled. One of them thought I was pointing into the deep-left-field stands and he said, "Who's what?"

"No, no," I said. "Who's this coming at us?" lowering my voice then and leaning in toward the reporters like a conspirator as the player loomed up. "Right here," I whispered as he passed just next to us. He looked up briefly and seeing the four of us staring at him from two or three feet away, he quickened his pace slightly.

"That guy?" one of them whispered.

"That's Bailey, for chrissake, Ed Bailey of Cincinnati," said the reporter who'd asked "Who's what?" He spoke petulantly as if he'd wished the question had tested him more severely. They were all looking at me. I hurried after the retreating catcher.

"Mr. Bailey," I said. He looked around, but kept walking.

I said in a rush: "I gotta pitch in a little while — a little too complicated to explain why — but I wondered if maybe you'd... well, if you'd warm me up."

He looked dubious. He said: "Nobody told me nothin'."

"It's really OK," I said.

He didn't seem assured; he began to stare around for someone to rescue him, I suppose, before he finally shrugged resignedly and together we headed for the plate near the third-base dugout where the visiting team's starting pitcher warms up before the game.

It was interesting throwing to him. He's out of a place called

Strawberry Plains, Tennessee, a big man, with a florid face, but he moves quickly and easily and pitching to him you felt it was impossible either to fool him, no matter how angry a spin you put on the ball, or to throw anything past him unless you threw the ball off at right angles. His big glove enveloped the ball. It was like throwing into a large mattress. He has the reputation in the National League of being a skillful talker behind the plate, wielding a patter like Yogi Berra's, the Yankee catcher, which can at its best distract the hitter. Bailey's special gift is his ability to get to Willie Mays. He makes him giggle shrilly. However, he said nothing to me. When he returned the pitches, the ball came back from him hard and accurate.

Beyond Bailey, behind the wire screen, a small knot of spectators craned to watch the trajectory of every pitch. That was another fine pregame pastime—ranked with watching the fungoes hit—to get behind the catcher during the warm-up and murmur judgment on the assorted flutters and breaks of big-league deliveries. My witnesses had little to exclaim about. I laid the pitches straight at Bailey's mitt, working easily and trying to get the windup and delivery smooth and effortless.

But then after a while I threw Bailey a curveball—a fine wide roundhouse that performed much better than I expected it to: it was thrown fast, off a wrist snap that shook the arm violently, and the ball swept and ducked across the plate at truly appreciable angles—across and down.

I don't know what the spectators behind the screen had to say about it. But Bailey's reaction was startling: quickly he reared up from his crouch.

"Hey!" he shouted. "Hey, kid, dammit when y'all throw the

hook, lemme know, hey?" His voice was high and disturbed. "Make a sign when y'all goin' to curve it." He gestured what he wanted me to do—a twist of the pitching hand—and then he fired the ball back hard, annoyed that I'd crossed him up.

The ball must have stung in the glove, but I hardly noticed. What I'd thrown had been recognized for what it was supposed to be. It was one of the great moments of the afternoon.

"Sure, sure," I yelled happily down at Bailey. "Absolutely!"

I threw a number of curves after that. The simple ritual of flashing the curve sign (which some pitchers do with a sweep of the glove) was irresistible. It seemed such a professional gesture that one did it timidly at first; but then after a while you got used to it, and the vanity of it, and also you took pride in giving the sign for the simple reason that it indicated a little variety in the repertoire. What the pitch did, or where it went—even if it behaved ignominiously and slithered in the grass—wasn't finally as meaningful as that preliminary nonchalant gesture of warning the catcher that a pitch was coming down that he'd better be on his toes about.

I warmed for about ten minutes. The arm felt good. Despite the number of times I gave the sign and threw the curve, I never got the big roundhouse to sweep over the plate with the authority of the first time I'd tried it. But I threw it with growing confidence until finally I promised myself that later on I would throw it against a major league batter to see what would happen to it.

I wanted to ask Bailey for a comment on my pitching ability, just on the off chance he might say something that would inspire confidence for the afternoon's labor. Pitchers need that sort of balm. Christy Mathewson once said, "A pitcher is not a ballplayer," and what he meant was that a pitcher is a specialist, an artist, with all the accompanying need of consolation and encouragement. Mollycoddling is almost as important to him as the rosin bag. One famous example of a pitcher's need for recognition was blurted into a microphone during the 1934 World Series by Detroit's hefty speedballer Schoolboy Rowe, the pitcher Dizzy Dean called pretty near as fast ("With a wind behind him") as his brother Paul. Rowe had a brilliant Series and following one victory he murmured over the radio to his wife, who was listening at home: "How'm I doing, Edna?" Detroit was playing the famous Gashouse Gang in that Series, and Dizzy Dean and the other St. Louis bench jockeys, including such violent and cackling tongues as Lippy Leo Durocher's, Pepper Martin's, K. O. Delancey's, and Ernie Showboat Orsatti's, never let Rowe forget that painful little phrase. Thereafter, he was inundated by the steamy chorus of "How'm I doing, Edna?" rising off the Cardinal bench.

In any case, I didn't ask Bailey for an opinion of my pitching, and he didn't offer one. After a while I called down to him that I'd had enough, and he turned without a word and went into the dugout.

When he'd gone, I looked out at the scoreboard. The distant clock hands stood almost at 1:30—the time Frank Scott had said we'd start.

It was obvious something was in the wind. The players were off the field, the reporters and photographers gone—the batting cage wheeled away and the groundskeepers sprucing up the pitcher's mound and around home plate. Both teams were standing by their dugouts. Some of the players seemed puzzled by the change in the pregame schedule. They talked among themselves. I saw a few fingers pointing, and also little quick gestures of the head in my direction to indicate that it was "that guy over there—the guy with the blue cap," and the eyes looking, and I felt the sweat start to seep in the palms—the fielder's mitt suddenly uncomfortably clammy and hot.

Then Frank Scott stepped briskly out toward the pitcher's mound. I watched him. Just across the base paths he wheeled and motioned me to follow him. It was obviously me he wanted.

I said, "Oh, Jesus," and I walked after him, across the white chalk of the foul lines which I was careful not to step on, and just before we reached the pitcher's mound he turned and faced me.

"OK," he said. "You're on."

It was exactly 1:30.

CHAPTER 11

———

When Scott pointed toward the first-base dugout and then made a circular motion with his arm upraised — like a squad leader signaling his men to assemble — the American League players started toward us. Being the home team they would be in the field first.

It was, in the vernacular, a pretty fair country ball club.

At first base was Mickey Vernon, twice winner of the American League batting championship and a very stylish and graceful fielder besides. He throws left-handed, which is, of course, a defensive advantage in a first baseman. He fits the general prescription for a first baseman — namely, that he should be long, lean, and left-handed. At second was Chicago's Nelson Fox — his round kewpie-doll face distorted by the big wad of "Favorite" tobacco he stuffs in his left cheek. He chewed licorice before he reached the big leagues, but his manager got him to change to chaws because the licorice made him sick. He swallowed his chaw on one hideous occasion he refuses either to disclose or discuss. He is a diminutive (150 pounds, 5 feet 8 inches) performer, yet brilliant enough both with the bat and in the field to win the

American League's Most Valuable Player Award the following year. His partner at second base was shortstop Billy Martin, the fiery ex-Yankee. He has a deceptively pleasant face, with melancholy brown eyes in it, and a long nose which got him into the early fights when his schoolmates ribbed him about it. It is a mobile face which has often worked hard and furiously an inch or so away from an umpire's. The Great Agitator, the press sometimes calls him, but he's more popularly known as the Kid, with—unlike me—the *k* capitalized, and he's a great favorite in the stadium. He was one of the few players who took a personal interest in my struggle that afternoon—sensing, I think, the loneliness and the awkwardness of being new and raw in a situation that in my case I could hardly hope to cope with skillfully. A spirited cockiness was his own defense. Riding into New York that first time, coming up on the long train ride from the St. Petersburg training camp, a reporter found him reading a magazine as the train moved into the Penn Station tunnel. Pretty excited about seeing New York for the first time? "Nah," said Martin, not yet then twenty. "I saw it in the movies." Nothing cowed him. He once told Ty Cobb, the legendary high-spike base runner and a noteworthy predecessor in what ballplayers call the "hard-nose" type of play, that he would've come into second base with his spikes up on the Kid only once. "After that," said Martin, "you would have had no teeth." It may have been a mask, this spirit, to hide the insecurity endured in a childhood of misery and poverty in the California town where he was raised, but it had made him, despite limitations as a ballplayer, a competitor whose drive picked up a whole team. Cobb liked him and grinned when he talked about him. He had such an excess of that competitive confidence that there seemed enough to pass around to his teammates—like pep pills. He tried to give me some of it. He kept up a steady chatter of encouragement while I was working—at least for a while—and I was grateful for it.

Down the line from Martin at third was Boston's Frank Malzone, silent while I toiled away, but the best man in the league at his position—sharp-featured, wiry, and fast. Durocher once appraised him: "The guy's got a fault? Dandruff, maybe." He's a wonderful defensive player who as the pitch is thrown leans in toward the batter in a pigeon-toed crouch. He has slightly bowed legs, and big feet, and when he poises on his toes to get a jump on the ball he looks like a flippered skin diver about to plunge off a rock. Behind him, out in left field, was Bob Cerv, who that year

"Chatting with Billy Martin in the dugout. Amused though he was by the perplexing nature of my assignment, I could sense his understanding and support throughout the afternoon." (*Garry Winogrand*)

had a brilliant season for the Athletics despite a fractured jaw which, being tightly wired for much of the season, limited his talk to the tight-lipped variety—whatever his mood—and required him to take sustenance—vegetable soups, orange juices, and such—through a tube stuck in a gap providentially left by a missing tooth in the side of his mouth. He'd lost weight that summer. He usually eats kolaches, big Bohemian meatballs, taking them at all meals, and at his usual playing weight he's powerfully heavy—a grim competitor with a hard, determined countenance marked by a nose flattened in a boyhood injury.

Playing over in right field was my friend of the batting cage, Harvey Kuenn, twice winner of the American League batting championship. A serious, unflamboyant professional, he keeps his baseball cap pulled down low over his eyes, so first you see the multifaceted Gothic D for Detroit embroidered on the front of the cap, then under the brim, the lower part of his face, severe, deeply burned, and, like Fox, with a chaw of tobacco tucked in the cheek. In center field was Mickey Mantle. Of all of them standing there, Mantle's was the power you sensed—seeing it in the heavy shoulders and arms sloping from a neck as thick as a water main. His large boyish face has gone heavy; he turns his head slowly, his eyes pale and impassive, so that there is something in his manner of the cat family: imperturbable, arch, and yet because the boyishness is still there he wears a faint expression of suspicious stubbornness, of petulance. The face of the final member of the team, my battery mate, the Yankees' Elston Howard, wore a puzzled frown because the reporters had been busy with him earlier—his exploits in left field during the World

Series, particularly one fine tumbling catch in the fifth game, made him copy as the World Series hero—and I don't believe anyone had had the chance to tell him why he was to put on his catching tools half an hour before the scheduled game. He hovered over Frank Scott, waiting for him to explain what we were all doing out there.

"Hey, Frank," someone said (it wasn't Howard), "what gives? What gives, man?"

Scott looked around to see that we were all there. Then he shuffled at some papers on a clipboard. "Well, boys...," he started to say.

At this point the recorded music which had been drifting in from center field stopped abruptly, in midchorus of "Tea for Two," then a stentorian cough came over the public-address system and we heard as follows:

"Your attention, please, (pause) George...P...P...P," then another pause, the announcer apparently working over a name scribbled on a pad, *"Prufrock,"* and then repeated with immeasurable confidence that boomed through the stadium, "George Prufrock *of* Sports Illustrated *will now pitch against the* entire *National League team, and the* entire *American League team... that team which collects the most hits to be awarded a prize of $1,000 by* Sports Illustrated."

"Well, there you are, boys," said Frank Scott. They were all looking at me. "That's the idea," he continued. "Four points awarded for the four-bagger, three for the triple, two for the double—you field first, through their first eight batters, and then you get your licks."

"You let 'em hit, kid," said Billy Martin. "And right at us, *pul-lease*, on the ground and in the big quick hops."

A few of the players laughed and someone said, "That's right, kid—you're out here to do the work; we're along for the ride," and around the circle they smiled again, trying to impart confidence, and as we stood together—waiting for something to happen to release us—I felt a sudden kinship with the players. It was an entirely unexpected emotion, since I was so obviously an outsider, but it came: that warm sense of camaraderie one gets, if briefly, as a team member, or in a platoon, or just sitting around a café with friends, never mentioned, but there nonetheless, almost tangible, and it was very strong before abruptly it was dissipated. Someone said, "OK, let's go," and the huddle broke up.

Surrounded by the players I had felt protected and grateful for my obscurity among them. But when they withdrew and headed for their positions, leaving me standing alone just off the mound, it was like being unveiled—and one sensed the slow massive attention of the spectators—by then almost 20,000 of them—wheel and concentrate, and almost physically I felt the weight of it. My palms were slick with sweat. I walked up on the pitcher's mound to find the rosin bag. There wasn't one there. A new ball was lying just off the pitcher's rubber. I picked it up but I didn't turn for the plate. I kept looking out at my infielders, trying to recapture the confidence I'd felt fleetingly in their company; they seemed very far away; they were busy scooping up grounders Vernon was lobbing to them from first base. When Malzone at third wound up and threw the ball, it was close enough to sigh past in a trajectory so flat that the ball never rose above eye level on its way into Vernon's glove. Out beyond the base paths, the outfielders had reached their positions. They were so far away I didn't feel we were identified with the same project. The spaces between them were vast. Everything seemed very peaceful and quiet out there. Deep back in the bleachers I could see a man, sitting up there alone, removing his coat to enjoy the afternoon sun.

I finally faced the plate. Howard was there waiting, his big dust-gray mitt up for the warm-up pitches. I threw him a couple. Then I wasn't conscious of the crowd. I'd forgotten that a pitcher, whatever his stature, concentrates on the strike zone to the exclusion of everything else. He's hardly ever conscious even of the batter, perhaps a bat waving in the vicinity of the strike zone. The crowd becomes a blur in the background. The noise it makes has a crisp quality, a sharp babble, since everybody's facing you, but it's impossible to distinguish its separate parts. Of course, if you listen for it, you can hear the Stevens vendors' *"HOT franks,"* "Hey, ICE-cream heah," and once I thought I heard Toots Shor yelling, but it isn't like sitting in the stands where you can hang on to four or five conversations at the same time. Mostly you hear your own voice—chattering away, keeping you company in the loneliness, cajoling and threatening if things begin to go badly, heavy in praise at times, much of everything being said half aloud, the lips moving, because although you know you're being watched, no one can hear you, and the sound of your voice was truly a steady influence—the one familiar verity in those strange circumstances. I recall the first sentence I spoke to myself was "OK, bo, you're goin' to be OK. Nothin' at all to worry about, nothin', nothin',", and at that moment, like a crack lawyer spring-ing to rebut, the public-address system announced the arrival at the plate of the National League's leadoff batter — Richie Ashburn.

He stepped into the batter's box wearing the bright candy-red pin-striped uniform of the Phillies. A left-handed batter, he punches at the ball, slapping it for a multitude of singles. The outfielders deploy for him like softball players. He chokes so far up on the bat that as he waited I could see his fingers flexing two or three inches up on the bat handle. He presented a surprisingly small target — as indeed all the batters seemed smaller than expected. Half consciously you expect them to rear high over the plate, threatening, portraits of power... but in fact their physical presence at the plate was not as overpowering as *recognizing* them — to look in and see under the batter's helmet a face which, jarringly familiar even from the pitcher's mound, one had only associated previously with newsprint and the photographs of the sports sections.

Behind the plate Howard had settled in his crouch, his big mitt up for the target. Concentrating on it, barely aware then of Ashburn, I toed the rubber with my spikes and with an almost physical jolt of will, I swung into a slow windup. Under the pres-sure of the moment I half expected to exhibit a pitching form as spastic as the cartwheeling fall of a man from a high tree. But conditioned reflexes took over, and I was surprised at the ease with which I got the pitch off. I was not prepared, however, for what then happened: that, rather than speeding for the bulk of Howard's catcher's mitt, the ball, flung with abandon and pro-pelled by a violent mixture of panic and pent-up anxiety let loose, headed straight for Ashburn's head. Down he went, flat on his back, the bat flung away, and an explosion of sound—a sharp gasp from the crowd—sailed out of the stands as I hurried off the mound calling out, "Sorry! Sorry!"

I ran halfway to the plate. The ball had shot by Ashburn, hit the edge of Howard's glove, and skidded off toward the stands. Ashburn picked himself up easily, collected his bat, and looked out at me calmly, his face imperturbable. He is one of the few players who doesn't lace his speech with cussing, his demeanor gentle, but I could think of nothing to say to him. So I shrugged— an inadvertent gesture that under the circumstances could only have indicated to Ashburn, and to Howard, standing peering at me through the bars of his mask, that I had no control whatsoever over my pitches. I did not look to see how the gesture was interpreted. I busied myself fielding a ball, a new one, someone had rolled out from the first-base dugout. Then I wheeled for the mound to try again.

I threw three more pitches to Ashburn, finding myself growing in confidence as I pitched. I threw him another ball, then a pitch that he chopped foul. On the next delivery he punched under the ball and lifted a high fly between third and home. Howard threw off his mask with a violence that rolled it almost to the backstop, and with shin guards clattering he went after the ball, got under it, and stomped around with his face upturned like a Paiute praying for rain until finally the ball came down and he smothered it in his big glove.

It took a few seconds, while the ball was being thrown around the infield, before there was any sense of accomplishment—it coming haltingly because, after all, one had expected devastation, not a harmless foul ball glinting in the sun, and finally it did come and I lurched happily in a tight circle around the pitcher's mound, digging and scraping at the dirt with my spikes, pretending preoccupation, and if there'd been a rosin bag I'd have picked it up and fussed briefly with it. What had seemed an inhospitable place, a steep uneven hill of dirt on which one moved gingerly and awkwardly, suddenly became something of a natural habitat—all around everything was familiar, neat, and orderly. But just as I began to admire the unmarked base paths, the bases unoccupied, with the fielders relaxed in their positions, a player with an established reputation for creating disorder in the pitcher's domain trotted up out of the National League dugout—San Francisco's Willie Mays.

I didn't see him at first. But from the stands a mounting roar of welcome greeted him. He'd been sorely missed in New York that summer, and the majority of the 20,000 were there in the hope of seeing him perform the miracles of play which would leave them breathless and cheering and yet a little guilty, too, to think that his ability, once practically a landmark in the city, was now on display elsewhere.

He gets set quickly at the plate, hopping eagerly into the batter's box, where he nervously jiggles and tamps his feet in the dust, twisting on his rear foot to get it solidly placed, staring down at the plate in concentration—to sense when his legs feel set—and when they do, he reaches out and taps the plate, twice, three times, with the bat before he sweeps it back over his right shoulder and cocks it. Then, for the first time, he looks out at the pitcher.

Most batters tuck their chins down and glower out at the pitcher from under the brims of their batting helmets—which makes them look properly sinister and threatening. Mays, on the other hand, who has a pleasant face to start with, looks out at the pitcher with a full, honest regard, his chin out, his eyes wide as if slightly myopic, and he seems to inspect the pitcher as if he was a harmless but puzzling object recently deposited on the pitcher's mound by the groundskeeper. Furthermore, when Mays's face is set in determination, his eyebrows arch up, so that under the batter's helmet his expression is a lingering look of astonishment, as if his manager had just finished addressing him at length in Turkish. But the deception is mild; you see the coiled power of his stance as he waits and the chances are that you'll turn away to look at something else.

I threw Mays three pitches. The motion felt easy and the first two pitches were low and didn't miss by much. With the third pitch, though, I was aware that the ball, almost as it left my hand, was heading accurately for the plate and that Mays, flexing his bat back to increase the purchase of his swing, was going to go for it. As his bat came through into the pitch, I could sense the explosive power generated and I flinched involuntarily—not sure that my hands, hung low and relaxed at the completion of the follow-through, didn't start up instinctively if futilely for protection. But from this flurry of power the ball rose straight, a foul ball like Ashburn's, I thought at first, but then I saw the ball carrying out over the infield. I had a glimpse of it high above me, small but astonishingly bright in the sunlight, directly above it seemed, and remembering that a pitcher leaves the fielding plays to his infielders I ran head down toward first base to vacate the mound for them.

I misjudged the ball badly. Actually, it came down back of the shortstop's position. Billy Martin was there to catch it and as I walked back to the mound, he threw the ball to Malzone, and the ball began to go from infielder to infielder—in that ritual of speeding the ball around the "horn" which gives the pitcher a moment to peek modestly out from under his cap and savor what he's just done. It was fine. It was truly all I could do to keep from grinning.

In recent years, in attempts to speed up the game, such rituals as throwing the ball around the infield have been considered dispensable by some authorities. Sadly, as the so-called deadweight components of the game are pruned away, it is always the pitcher who suffers. The authorities want to limit mound conferences. A few of the more impatient umpires yell at a dawdling pitcher that his pants aren't falling off, his cap is straight—to quit fussing with them and pitch. In some parks, rather than waste the time he takes walking in from the bullpen, a relieving pitcher is transported to the mound in a whitewall-tired automobile. In Boston's Fenway Park they have a scooter. The pitcher looks uncomfortable sitting there with a glove on his lap; beside him, the chauffeur is usually grinning—as if delivering a man in particularly ludicrous costume to a charity ball. Actually, the pitcher as the prima donna of the baseball roster needs that long walk from bullpen to pitcher's mound: his vanity delights in the picture he presents as a lonely but courageous figure, his jacket carefully shielding the pitching arm, tramping his way in past the outfielders as his name is bellowed out over the loudspeaker system. It means he can play the part of the avenging angel without actually doing anything but walking — at least for the moment. The pitcher is happiest with his arm idle. He prefers to dawdle in the present, knowing that as soon as he gets on the mound and starts his windup he delivers himself to the uncertainty of the future. Similarly, the ritual of throwing the ball around the infield allows the pitcher to postpone the future; it allows him to fuss around on his hill of dirt like a gawky hen; he can pick up and drop the rosin bag; he's given a moment or so in which to preen himself on his accomplishments. It is the fine moment of his profession. It was certainly the fine moment of my afternoon. When Mays hit that towering fly and it was evident it was going to be caught, I stood absorbing that October instant so that it would be forever available for recall — now blurred, of course, and fragmentary like the nickelodeon films of the Dempsey-Firpo fight you see in the amusement parks, but still sufficient to put one back there on the mound: seeing again, and feeling the sudden terror of Mays uncoiling his bat, but then watching in surprise the ball rise clean and harmless, Billy Martin circling under it, hooded and efficient with his sunglasses down, catching it then and removing it from his glove to peer at it as if he'd never seen a baseball before, then firing it down to Malzone, who also looked at it, across then to Vernon for his inspection, and during this you felt coming on a maniac grin of achievement which you had to control, knowing that pitchers don't grin after getting a man out, so you solemnly stomped around the mound, tidying it up, watching with sidelong glances the ball whip from infielder to infielder, the great blue-shadowed humming tiers of the stadium out of focus beyond, until finally you remember Nelson Fox, the big orange-size chaw pushing out the side of his face, trotting in to the mound, looking at the ball in his hand, jiggling it, inflicting it with magic, then popping it in the air at you and saying, "Come on, kid, easy, easy, easy."

That is all of that day that I really care to remember. Perhaps a bit more: that when I got the ball from Fox it felt familiar to the hand, a weapon suddenly adaptable, an instrument perfectly suited to my design. Of course, I should have known better. Polishing the ball, the glove slung on the wrist, I turned on the mound and saw Frank Robinson, the great Cincinnati slugger, standing in the batter's box, and I knew then that the pitcher's pleasure is a fragmentary thing, that the dugouts, like sausage machines, eject an unending succession of hitters to destroy any momentary complacency a pitcher may feel during an afternoon of work.

Regardless, as I looked in at Robinson—Howard behind him adjusting his mask—I thought, Well, why not, I've done pretty well so far—now's the time to unleash the curveball, the hook. And perhaps if the hook works, I'll chance the change of pace and maybe even the knuckler. Given the opportunity I knew it would be unforgivable not to try all the pitches in my repertoire; and so, swallowing hard, nervous again after the heady triumph of retiring the first two batters, I worked my fingers around the seams until I had the ball held properly for the curve. Robinson, the victim, was standing easily in the batter's box; Howard had settled into his position, his glove raised as a target. I remembered then Ed Bailey's stern charge to indicate when a curve was coming up; but I didn't see how I could tell Howard without tipping off Robinson. My catcher would have to fend for himself as best he could, I thought, and I pumped my arm twice and swung into the windup.

CHAPTER 12

In baseball parlance they speak of a pitch "getting away" from the pitcher. As I came through the delivery of my curve, I failed to snap my wrist sufficiently and my hook got away from me in majestic style—sailing far over both Robinson's and Howard's heads to the wire screen behind home plate. If it had hit a foot or so higher, the ball would have caught the netting of the foul screen and run up it to the press boxes. It was such an extraordinarily wild pitch that I felt I had to make some comment; what I'd done was too undignified to pass unnoticed, and so once again I hurried off the mound calling out, "Sorry! Sorry!" Howard and Robinson gazed out at me, both startled, I think, perhaps even awed by the strange trajectory of my pitch, which was wild enough to suggest that I had suddenly decided to throw the ball to someone in the stands. The embarrassment was intense. Afterward I made some inquiries as to how that pitch of mine compared with some of the wilder heaves around the majors. Perhaps I would have felt better if I'd known that, while my curve may have been one of the tallest thrown, it certainly wasn't the wildest. In an exhibition game Chuck Stobbs, for example, the Washington left-hander, nearly brained Alvin Dark, who was kneeling in the on-deck circle a good sixty or seventy feet off the plate; Stobbs lost his grip on the ball during his windup and since there were men on base he had to go through with his pitch or commit a balk. The ball shot past Dark, who didn't say a word; he stared briefly out at the mound and then he clapped on his batter's helmet. On another occasion, Stobbs — who seems to have a propensity for this sort of thing — bumped the ball against his side during the windup and threw it off his fingertips into the seventeenth row of the grandstand. He counted off those rows afterward. He said he didn't know whether to laugh or cry.

My own reaction was one of such embarrassment at seeing that pitch sail off that my repertoire was immediately reduced to the simple fastball. Later I was accused of throwing another curveball, but I could not have done so intentionally. I stuck to the fastball for the rest of the afternoon.

It took me a few pitches to steady down after the attempted hook. Finally I threw a pitch Robinson found to his liking. He is a thin, long-boned player who hangs his head over the plate to watch the pitch coming in. He has wonderful wrists, strong, supple, and in St. Louis he once sprained his wrists while checking his swing — which would indicate both his power and his speed of reaction. He brought his hands around on the sixth pitch I threw him (a friend in the stands acting as statistician was keeping track) and it was over the plate and chest high. Often a pitcher has a premonition as soon as the ball leaves his hand that the batter is going to feast on it. He sees the bat flex back and instinctively he knows that the batter's timing is right, that the ball's not going to do anything to escape the sweep of the bat coming through, and as it *does* he hears the sharp disheartening *whack* of ash against the ball and the drive lines out past his ears. In Robinson's case, the ball soared between Mantle and Cerv in deep-left-center field, dropped between them, and rolled for the Babe Ruth memorial out by the flagpole. By the time the ball was back in the infield, Robinson was standing on second.

The public-address system announced "two points for the National League" and Robinson, his job done, trotted in from second base.

Actually, it didn't feel too disheartening, that double, because Robinson didn't stay on base to remind you of it. If he'd been leading off second, swaying his body, poised for flight, and you had to work off the stretch, peering around and worrying about him, you would have had the evidence of your inadequacy as a pitcher right there nagging at you. Perhaps the one, if very slight, compensation for the pitcher who has a home run hit off him is that it leaves the bases uncluttered of the opposition and in the pristine state the pitcher prefers. His dismay may be intense watching the ball fly out of the park, but at least it is temporary: the batter circles the bases and is back in the obscurity of the dugout within seconds.

So I didn't have to worry about a man jiggling up and down the base paths. But there was something else bothering me as I watched Ernie Banks, the home run king of the National League, step out of the on-deck circle and head for the plate. Of the six pitches I'd thrown to Robinson one or two had seemed to me to catch the strike zone. He hadn't gone for them, and there was no umpire to contradict his choice.

I hadn't arranged for an umpire for the simple reason that I didn't trust my control. Often, during those nervous days just before my appearance in the stadium, I'd had a recurrent presentiment of losing control of my pitches and having an umpire award an unending succession of bases on ball. Such nightmarish things did, after all, happen even in the major leagues. Not long ago, Ray Scarborough, a pitcher on the Washington Senators, after giving up seven runs in the first inning of his first appearance in the majors, which was against the Yankees, started against the Red Sox soon after and walked the first seven men he faced. Bucky Harris was his patient manager at the time, and when the seventh batter tossed aside his bat and started trotting down to first, he walked out to Scarborough and reached for the ball. "Son," he is supposed to have said mildly. "I think maybe we've had our workout for the day, don't you?"

Under the peculiar setup of my pitching stint, if there'd been rigid rulings on balls and strikes, I might easily have eclipsed Scarborough's feat, and found myself, as a result, standing uneasily in the magazine office downtown after the game trying to explain what I'd done for the $1,000 — namely, that I'd enjoyed the opportunity of walking every man I'd faced — which would have been a total of sixteen.

So I made no arrangements about umpires.

I didn't consider, however, the possibility that the batters — and quite properly since money was at stake — would get finicky about the pitches and wait for one they felt they could get a "holt" of — as they say. Even if a pitch was in the strike zone, they could let it go by if they felt uncomfortable about it without any fear of penalty — without an umpire screaming *stee-rike* in their ears.

However, as I stood on the mound watching Banks set himself at the plate, I wasn't overly worried. After all, I'd thrown thirteen pitches to three batters, which indicated the control was reasonable, and not bad pitching—considering who was throwing them—even if one of them had nearly beaned a batter, another was probably the tallest curve ever thrown in Yankee Stadium, and the last one Robinson had smacked for a stand-up double.

I had a grand opportunity to study Banks. Or, rather, Banks was up at the plate for such a long time that for days afterward a slight and regretted tug at the memory would unveil him clear in my mind's eye: a right-handed batter, slender, standing very quietly back in the farthest recesses of the batter's box with none of the nervous fidgeting of a Mays or a Ted Williams, his bat steady and cocked up vertically behind his right ear, rarely leveled out in a practice swing as he waited with his eyes peering out calmly from beneath the Cubs' outsize and peaked cap. His whole attitude was of such detachment that I found it unnerving to pitch to him. Once in a while he'd step out of the batter's box and, resting his bat against his knees, he'd slowly pour dust from one palm to the other before settling back in with an attitude of faint disdain, as if in his opinion the pitcher's stature was that of a minor functionary whose sole duty was to serve up a fat pitch.

As it happened, a fat pitch was certainly what Banks wanted. He won a Most Valuable Player Award for his performance that year, crediting his success to his ability to lay off the bad pitches. An excellent habit, obviously, and he had no intention of breaking it as he stood in against me. I threw him a total of twenty-three pitches. There may not have been an umpire to judge their quality, but it was certain that Banks found very few to his liking. Sometimes he would lean over and watch the ball right into Howard's glove, then look up with a small encouraging smile, as if to indicate that it was close—that if the pitch had been a shade nearer the center of the plate, why, he would have whipped his bat around. Occasionally he would foul a pitch off into the stands, and from the first-base dugout someone would roll a new ball out to the mound; I'd pick it up, stalk back onto the mound, gaze mournfully at Banks, concentrate then on the bulk of Howard's catcher's mitt, crank up, and let fly. As I worked away, my control began to vanish under the pressure. My sense of well-being, not bothered by Robinson's double, began to deteriorate; I started to talk to myself loudly; the mound, the pitching rubber, previously so familiar, quickly became alien ground that I stumbled over and couldn't get the feel of with my spikes; the baseball itself seemed noticeably heavier, the seams awry; the whole process of throwing a baseball with accuracy became an absurdly hard task, and as I pitched, Banks seemed to recede into the distance, along with Howard, until the two of them looked like figures viewed through the wrong end of a telescope.

What does a pitcher do when things begin to collapse around him? Almost surely he looks for assistance, someone to trot in to the mound and minimize his difficulties, to bolster him with encouragement. If the situation indicates that his skill has leaked away under the pressure, he expects his manager to come out and replace him. I remember Bob Turley, the great Yankee speed pitcher, describe a jam he'd manufactured for himself in the 1955 World Series—the first Series game he ever played in. He loaded the bases in the first inning and had Roy Campanella to face.

Fidgeting, trying to pull himself together by breathing in great gulps of air, Turley turned and looked hopefully out at the bull-pen. Nothing was going on. He peered into the dugout. His manager, Casey Stengel, was sitting with his legs crossed, leaning forward and looking up at the box where the Yankee owners were sitting. Turley had one quick image of working in Washington the next season—then the ultimate penalty for ineptitude. But then Yogi Berra came waddling out toward him from the plate, and Turley felt better. At last, he thought, I'm going to be all right because here comes Yogi to give me some advice. "Boy," Turley reported Berra as saying when he reached the mound, "boy, you're in one *helluva* jam."

The gravity of my situation with Ernie Banks was compounded by not having anyone I could turn to. Even such cold words of comfort as Berra offered Turley would have been welcome; but Elston Howard, my catcher, cared so little for the business at hand—having a full game to catch later on—that often if my pitches were out of the strike zone, or in the dust, he'd let them skip by without budging for them and the balls would thud ignominiously against the backstop. Howard is a serious competitor and very studious about his play. One winter he spent hours working on his batting stance, swinging at a ball suspended from a wire in the basement of his home. I don't think he was at all clear why he was engaged in this pregame malarkey. Occasionally he would rise from his position behind the plate, turn to the dugout, and shrug his shoulders in a massive pantomime of bewilderment. Once I heard him shout to someone in the dugout, "Hey, gettin' bushed out here"—referring to himself.

Naturally there wasn't anyone in either dugout I could

complain to—neither teammates nor even a manager. In fact, it struck me then that if I went completely to pieces there was no one to relieve me. Until my grandiose scheme to pitch to both leagues was fulfilled, I was doomed to toil away—condemned, as someone pointed out later, to a curious modern adaptation of the myth of Sisyphus, the unfortunate Greek whose endless task it was to push a boulder to the top of a mountain only to have it topple from his grasp. The only encouragement I had was the faint, apologetic smile of Banks himself. A quick, embarrassed look around my infield was no help. Their faces were averted: Mickey Vernon was looking solemnly into his first baseman's glove; the others were either preoccupied with their shoe tops or scratching with their spikes in the dirt of the base paths. In the outfield I caught one awful glimpse of Mickey Mantle—turned toward one of the other outfielders and patting his mouth in an ostentatious yawn to show his boredom.

I turned hurriedly from that spectacle, rushed up on the mound, and began spraying pitches in at Banks as if by sheer volume I'd get one where he'd swing away. Occasionally the fouls would lift lazily into the stands and out of the corner of my eye I'd glimpse the people in that section rise, their arms outstretched, and the ball would fall in, engulfed like a pebble tossed into a field of wheat.

I asked my statistician, Bob Silvers, after the game what the spectators' reaction had been during the time of my troubles with Banks, and he said they took it very calmly—more calmly certainly than the febrile activity on the mound suggested I was taking it. He jotted down the following conversation between two men sitting in the sun in their shirtsleeves, one of them wearing a straw hat.

"Hey, who's that guy?"

"What guy?"

"Guy pitching."

"Donno. Some guy called Prufrock."

"Which?"

"Prufrock!"

"Who the hell's Prufrock?"

"Beats me."

Each sentence was followed by a long pause, while the beer was sipped from the big paper cups, the mind just barely ticking over in that splendid October sun.

Finally, on pitch number 23, Banks lifted a high fly ball out to Mickey Mantle in right-center field, who was not so busy yawning that he didn't see the ball arch out toward him, and standing on the mound I saw he was going to catch it, and I gave a big shuddering sigh of relief to think that no longer did I have to look in to see Banks standing there with those red-striped blue socks high on his legs, his small head leaning over the plate, the thin smile...and when he came up after the game and we joked about it I told him that one of the lasting impressions of that afternoon would be the relief I felt watching him trudge back to the dugout, trailing his bat along behind him as if it had become heavy during that long stay of his at the plate.

CHAPTER 13

———

Ernie Banks was followed in the batter's box by Frank Thomas, then playing for the Pittsburgh Pirates. He was the only batter I faced who loomed over the plate. Despite a large, homely, friendly face over which his blue plastic helmet perched like a birthday paper hat, Thomas's size made him look dangerous; he had an upright batting stance, which made him easier to pitch to than Banks, but the bat looked small and limber in his hands, and when he swung and missed one of my first pitches to him I imagined I heard the bat sing in the air like a willow switch. For the first time the batter's box seemed close, and I could understand why many pitchers manipulate the follow-through of their pitching motion, which brings them in toward the plate by as much as six feet, so that the glove can be flicked up to protect the head in the event of a hard shot toward the mound. You never can tell. In 1947 Schoolboy Rowe threw in a pitch toward Stan Musial and back came the top half of a bat cracked directly in two, whirring at him with the speed and directness of a boomerang, and struck him a brutal blow on the elbow of his upflung arm. Even batters worry about crippling a pitcher over that distance. A hard-hit line drive, after all, will cover those 60 feet 6 inches in a sixth of a second. Babe Ruth had nightmares of such a thing, and there's a body of thought which believes his fear of smacking down a pitcher was why he changed his batting style (he was originally a line-drive hitter in the early days with Baltimore) and started swinging from the heels of his pipestem legs to get loft and distance.

According to my statistician in the stands, it was the seventh pitch that Thomas whacked in a long high arc, very much like that of a Ruthian home run, deep into the upper deck in left field. The ball looped in at the downward end of its trajectory and above the swelling roar of the crowd I could hear it smack against the slats of an empty seat. The upper deck was deserted and it was a long time before a scampering boy, leaping the empty rows like a chamois, found the ball and held it aloft, triumphant, the white of it just barely visible at that great distance.

The ball was hit well over four hundred feet and after the roar that had accompanied its flight had died down, you could hear the crowd continue buzzing.

My own reaction, as I stood on the mound, was not one of shame, or outrage. Perhaps it should have been, particularly following my difficulties with Banks, but actually my reaction was one of wonderment at the power necessary to propel a ball out of a major league park. I could hardly believe a ball could be hit so far.

Later that afternoon in the locker room I asked Billy Pierce, the great White Sox southpaw, about the effect of the home run on the pitcher. He'd been talking about the major league curveball, what a marvelous and wicked weapon it was at its best, and the unwelcome shift into the batter's province threw him off. "Home runs?" he said in a high, querulous voice. He shrugged. "Well, the effect of the damn things depends upon their importance in any given game," he said reflectively. "Look at Branca." He thought for a while and then he said: "But when that ball sails out of the park, even if it doesn't mean a damn thing, you just feel awful stupid."

Pierce's mention of Branca, of course, was in reference to Bobby Thomson's home run off the Brooklyn speed pitcher in the Miracle of Coogan's Bluff play-off game in 1951. In the films of that stupendous moment you see Branca wheel to watch the flight of the ball that lost Brooklyn the pennant, then start slowly for the dugout, but almost running finally to get out of that wild public demonstration into privacy where he could project that scene over and over again in his imagination, never quite believing it, puzzled that the script wouldn't change and the ball curve foul or into an outfielder's reach. An enterprising photographer got into the Dodger dressing room—it was barred to the press but he got in somehow—and took a picture of Branca within minutes of his disaster. The photograph, a strange one, shows him facedown and prostrate on a flight of cement steps—as if he'd stumbled on the bottom step and fallen face forward, his body absolutely as stiff as cordwood with grief. The effect of that home run finished Branca, practically speaking, as a pitcher. Afterward he toyed with the idea of changing his uniform number, which was 13, but he never did. Perhaps he knew that nothing would help him.

I found I couldn't explain the effect of Frank Thomas's home run, at least not to Pierce, because in actual fact I felt a certain sense of pride in that home run. Every time I return to Yankee Stadium—to a football game, for example—I automatically look up into the section where the ball hit, it was section 34, remembering then that I felt no sense of stupidity but in fact enjoyed a strong feeling of identification with Thomas's feat—as if I was his partner rather than opposing him, and that between us we'd connived to arrange what had happened. It was as if I'd wheeled to watch the ball climb that long way for the upper deck and called out, "Look, look what I've helped engineer!"

It wasn't a reaction I could have explained to Pierce without being accused of being in sympathy with the enemy. Besides, he was back on pitchers, talking about curveballs, the gloomy consideration of Branca, and the batter and his prowess postponed, laid away in the shadows, as he described a bright and cheerful world full of pitching splendors.

"You've got to see Donovan's curve," he said eagerly. "Can't tell about the curve on TV. Got to catch it, try to catch it, to see what the thing does. It breaks so you can almost hear it."

So we talked comfortably about pitching. I told him that I'd thrown one curveball that afternoon. "It was the first pitch I threw to Frank Robinson," I said. "It almost ran up the foul screen. It got away from me."

"I see," said Pierce. "So *that's* what it was."

Later that afternoon, Gil Hodges, the Dodger first baseman, complained that I had thrown him a curveball. He followed Thomas in the lineup and, despite the fact that he hit the curveball for a sharp single to short center, he spoke to me reproachfully. He told me he didn't think curveballs were allowed.

I was surprised at the high respect major leaguers hold for the curveball and how they hate to bat against it. If a curve is hit safely, the batter attributes his success less to his own ability than to being given the chance to take advantage of a fault in the curve itself. "That hook hung up there just long enough," he will say later in the dugout, meaning that he was able to get his bat around on the ball before it broke. Any player who professes to prefer taking his swipes against curveballs is looked upon with suspicion. And indeed in the history of the majors only a few players have had the reputation of preferring to see curves thrown at them: Hornsby, for one, Rollie Hemsley, Moose Skowron, Roy Sievers, Ducky Medwick, and Al Simmons, these last two despite both having the fault of stepping away from the pitch with the forward foot, falling away "into the bucket"—supposedly suicidal against the curve. They compensated for their faulty swings with amazing eyes and quick strong wrists. There are others, of course, who do well against curveball pitchers, but nonetheless the curve has always been better known for destroying reputations. Jim Thorpe, for example, probably the greatest athlete who ever lived, never stuck in the majors because a curveball fooled him too often. A rookie's classic letter from the training camp begins: "I'll be home soon, ma. The pitchers are starting to curve me."

Frankly, I don't remember throwing Hodges a curveball. But I remember other things about his lengthy tenure at the plate, right from the beginning as he stepped into the batter's box, hitching up his baseball pants, reaching out then and rubbing up the fat part of his bat as he set himself, picking again at those pants as if about to wade into a shallow pond. He has outsize hands, which you notice when he stands in at the plate. They span over twelve inches, and Peewee Reese, his captain, used to say of him, in connection with those big hands, that he only used a glove for fielding at first base because it was fashionable. They call him Moon, and I remember how he looked, the rather beefy pleasant face under the blue helmet, and the blue piping of the Dodger uniform, and while I don't remember throwing him a curve, I remember the line-drive single he hit, how easy and calculated his swing, and how sharp that hit of his was going out... but mainly I remember something else.

CHAPTER 14

I t was while Hodges was at the plate that the inner voice, which had been mumbling inaudibly at first, and calmly, began to get out of control. On the pitcher's mound one was conscious not of the hum of the crowd or even, closer at hand, the encouragement of the infielders. What you remembered was this voice chattering away within your head, offering comfort, encouragement, advice. I was acutely aware of this separation of mind and body: the mind seemed situated in a sort of observation booth high above the physical self, which, clumsy and ill equipped in these unnatural surroundings, took on the aspect of an untrustworthy machine—a complicated cranelike bipedal mechanism sporting two jointed appendages, one of which with a rusty creak of rarely used parts was supposed to hurl a horsehide spheroid 60 feet 6 inches with accuracy. That was the function of the physical plant, and high above, peering down like a skeptical foreman, the mental self offered a steady commentary which reflected how well the machine was doing.

I don't pretend there is anything remarkable about this dichotomous condition. Such mumbling is familiar to all of us. During the 1958 World Series television gave the country a remarkable opportunity to watch a ballplayer talking to himself, often the telescopic lenses bringing you so close to him that you felt you were going to overhear him. He was the Milwaukee pitcher Lew Burdette, the big West Virginian from an explosives center called Nitro. In those television close-ups you'd see his mouth working as he chatted to himself out there on the pitcher's mound, and while there were some skeptics who took him to be simply at work churning up the wherewithal for his controversial spitball, it was obvious, at least, that if he was preparing such a mixture to treat the ball he was talking to himself at the same time.

Not long after the Series, and my own experience in Yankee Stadium, I wrote Burdette a brief letter—asking him if in the interests of a magazine article he would disclose what he says to himself on the pitcher's mound. I enclosed a self-addressed envelope, stamped and all, just as we did back when we wrote away for autographs, and sent it to the Braves' office in Milwaukee. Something must have gone wrong. Some weeks later a reply came—but not actually a reply since what I took out of the envelope on a cold winter's day was a single sheet of paper with six or seven Braves' autographs on it. I'm not even sure (having lost the paper since) that Burdette's name was among them.

Often I imagine that my letter was forwarded properly and that Burdette got it, and sat down and took considerable pains to answer the request, but that somehow he tucked his reply in the wrong envelope. And then I think of the recipient—a youngster in Appleton, Wisconsin, say, just finishing his first year in Little League, baseball his passion, and writing away to his hero, Burdette, for his autograph, and any of his teammates' if it wasn't too much bother, and then blocking in a few painfully wrought sentences of how he was dreaming of pitching one day in County Stadium, and working on his control and all…and how weeks later the reply came—the three-page typewritten letter signed by the great Burdette himself and starting off politely: "Thank you for your interest in what I say to myself…" and how the boy had walked along the cold country road trying to read it, puzzling over the long words like "self-criticism" and "provocation" and the short ones such as "id" and "ego," and how he'd taken it to bed with him and looked at it under the covers with a flashlight, learning nothing, not quite sure he oughtn't to show it to a higher authority, his parents perhaps, and even, frankly, a little worried now about his association with Little League.

There have been other chattering pitchers (it seems a habit restricted to that position)—Tommy Byrne for one. He was a tall, stooped figure who toiled for the Yankees in the early fifties—a more voluble talker, even, than Burdette. Sometimes you could hear him all over the park, not so much talking to himself as offering a general running commentary to anyone within earshot: his infielders, the batter, the crowd. Often, if a batter listened carefully, he'd hear Byrne say, "Gonna throw you a hook, mistah," and sometimes he'd get one and sometimes he wouldn't. The ballplayers had a fine name for Byrne. "The Broadcaster" they called him, and Casey Stengel, whose own famous brand of talk invariably seems an extension of the subconscious, was so genuinely fond of him that he kept him around much longer than his ability called for. There are others: Ed Plank, the great procrastinator, a fidgeter who took so long staring in at the plate that a batter's eyes would water waiting for the pitch to come down, who before beginning his motion would further dismay the batter by discussing him audibly: *Easy man. No hit. One down, two to go. Nobody hits.* More recently Jim Brosnan, the bespectacled relief pitcher who refers to the inner voice as Silent Screaming in his valuable chronicle *The Long Season,* occasionally erupts vocally: *Ils ne passeront pas,* he is said to have mumbled at a startled batter.

In any athletic contest we urge ourselves on in some fashion of this sort or other. In rare cases, the inner voice actually takes on a physical form. Arthur Larsen, the national tennis champion in 1950, believed he was being advised and cajoled throughout a match by a large eagle that perched on his shoulder. Larsen had a habit that one remarked on if one saw him play enough — a slight twist of the head just before he served...as if he was trying to rid himself of a crick in the neck. What he was doing was turning his head so the eagle could speak more directly into his ear. I assume his imaginary eagle took off when the point started and hovered above the court, taking reconnaissance during play, to swoop down when the point was over and spill what it had learned in Larsen's ear.

My own voice never took on a guise as esoteric as that of an eagle. It had no form; it just chatted away from limbo as normally as it could under the circumstances. During the first moments on the pitcher's mound, as Richie Ashburn set himself at the plate, it occupied itself with the general urging to "calm down and take it easy" — but you felt the hypocrisy nonetheless...the hysteria lurking close at the edge of the voice, like a hyena beyond the firelight, and the mouth was very dry.

After the astonishing success with Richie Ashburn and Willie

Mays, their high flies both caught in the infield, the voice became almost uncontrollable with delight. In its pleasure at the machine under observation it cried out to it "How t'*go,* bébé!" and "Boy, you *kid!*" and also there bounced around within my head such strange effusive exclamations as "Gol-*ding* it!" and "Gee-*zus!*" and when the grin tried to spread across the face it was in reaction to this close harmony between body and spirit.

So successful was the machine during its early operation that for a while the inner voice took scant notice that quickly thereafter the machine's performance began to suffer. After the debacle of the curve thrown to Frank Robinson, high over his head and almost up the screen behind home plate, and the subsequent line-drive double, the inner voice still remained chipper and confident— booming phrases back and forth within the skull as hearty as late-afternoon conversation in the locker room of a golf club. "You doin' just *fine,* heah? Just fine," it would say—for mysterious reasons of its own with a Southern inflection. It wasn't until Ernie Banks's extended presence at the plate that the voice's tone became somewhat more shrill and panicky. Still, it remained under control. It offered advice: "Y'all *pushing* the ball, bo," it would say. "Don't push the ball like that, all stiff-like...easy *does* it, bo," and then quite often during the windup it would say: "OK now Mistah Banks, y'all gonna swing at this pitch, you heah? OK? Now heah she comes, please m'boy, *swing* at it, SWING AT IT...Oh chrissake, hey, what's wrong with y'all, Mistah Banks, can't y'all *see?*" this last in a high whine as Elston Howard would retrieve the ball from the dust where he'd blocked it and whip it back.

It was during Banks's tenure that the inner voice refused to stay contained within the head. The lips began to move and my mumbled voice became increasingly audible on that lonely hill, mooning and squeaking like the fluttery breath of a tuckered hound.

"Lookit that thing go on *out* theah!" it gasped when Banks had finally gone, and Frank Thomas's long home run started for the depths of the upper deck. *"Lawd Almighty!"*

The voice still wasn't strained with gloom, however, or even edgy following that tremendous blow; it was assessing the situation, and while there was awe in its tone and breathlessness, along with that strange Southern cracker inflection, it was a sturdy voice, and it would have been hard to guess that within four minutes or so that same voice would crack under the strain.

What caused it to crack was a string of seven balls I threw to Gil Hodges before he hit three fouls in a row and then his single, none of these first pitches close enough to the plate to get him to so much as twitch the bat off his shoulder. At first the voice offered its usual counsel not to push the ball and to take things easy; presently it got exasperated—"Hey, come on now, bear *down,* Ah say"—like a short-tempered farmer training a pup to come to heel; then finally, as the control continued to flag, the panic surged in not by degrees but coming quickly, like a prowler's bulk suddenly filling a doorway, and it came in and throttled the voice so that all that came out was a thin high squeak.

And then this curious thing happened. *It turned traitor.* The voice went defeatist on me. It escaped and ran off, washing its hands of the whole miserable business. But it didn't desert me completely. Much worse, it capered around out there on the periphery—jeering and catcalling. "You fat fool!" it would call out, not concerned that the object of its raillery was splinter-thin, and, with the sweat pouring off, getting thinner. "You po' fat *fool*...y'think y'all pretty fat and *smart* standing out theah pitching, hey? Well, lemme tell yo' sumpin. Y'all can't pitch yo' way out of a paper bag, that's what. Jes' try. Jes' le's see yo' *try* putting the ball ovah the plate."

So I would try—and when the ball missed the strike zone under Hodges's watchful eye, the voice would cackle gleefully: "Y'all see that? Oh *my!* Y'all see that ball roll in the dust? Ladies an' gen'men, d'yall *observe* that ball drop down theah in the dirt. Haw! Haw! Haw!" it would roar gustily in my head. "Haw! Haw! Haw!"

Afterward I thought about that bellowing turncoat voice, bewildered by it, and ashamed until for a while I decided that its traitorous conduct was just another way of blowing off steam. After all, in moments of severe stress the voice often lets go like a wayward rocket. In many European sports it's not considered indecorous to explode—particularly in the Latin countries where a player's emotional state at such times will range from the quiet sobbing of the pelota player, his basket drooped like a broken wing, leaning his head against the stone wall of the court and bewailing his errors, to the tumultuous demonstrations of the soccer player who will often hurl himself to the ground, kick, and snatch at tufts of grass with his teeth.

It isn't only the Latins. I know a Westchester commuter who plays squash in a New York athletic club with a grim, voluble ferocity which reaches its peak when in his crisis of frustration he lets loose a throbbing scream of anguish—usually after missing a shot, but sometimes, as I say, just to let the pressure go—a lash

of sound that beats on the ear like a wall of surf, jolting the players in the other courts to jump as if seawater boiled at their
ankles, and then that wash of noise booms into the dressing room
where in the cubicles they grin and say, "Well, ol' Larry's really
lettin' loose today...the Screamer must be taking a shellacking,"
and pours down the wide carpeted stairs to inundate the leather
armchairs below, and the smoking stands, and the backgammon
tables, and the tall clocks with the great pendulums that move
slowly as the rock of an ocean liner, and in the distant library the
old men stir from their sleep and blink under the pale thin sheets
of the *Wall Street Journal* drawn up over their heads, and on a
good clear day, with Larry in full throat, that wave of sound
reaches three floors down to the ground level below and the thin
tatters of it curl out into the street like wisps of scud.

Perhaps that voice of mine, cavorting on the distant sidelines,
yelling its scorn through cupped hands, was a manifestation of
this sort—as meaningless and harmless as my friend's high-
pitched anguish. I thought so for a while. But then a month later
I changed my mind. I found out that if your faculties don't stay
around to help you, it simply means you're inadequate to the
task, running from it shamefully. I was playing bridge with three
great experts as part of my proposed series for *Sports Illustrated;*
my partner was Oswald Jacoby, a gruff, big, round-shouldered
genius with small pudgy hands that hold his cards in sloppy
clumps which he scowls at from a face twisting in the agues and
tics of concentration, his brain—legend has it—one of those
that cracked the Japanese naval code...and this man, my partner, a grim competitor, was so outraged at a bad mistake of mine
that he rose up from his chair, heavily, like a broaching whale,

and shouted among other things: "What-did-you-do-that-for? Why? Why? Why?"

I didn't know. I didn't know when I looked up and saw Jacoby rearing up from the other side of the table as big in his rage as a cliff. My whole mental being fled before him like a frightened crow. This time the voice didn't even stay around to jeer. It offered the slightest sound: "Donno," it said, as forlorn as the cry of a bird in a petrified forest, and then it got out and kept on going. It never stopped, and just as it had been in the stadium, the physical self was left to face the music alone, disembodied and empty of mind, nothing for it to do but pluck feebly along the edge of the card table with its fingers.

CHAPTER 15

My statistician had some further notes on those two men sitting in front of him. One of them had put a white handkerchief around his neck to protect it from the sun, and they sat relaxed, slowly rocking the beer around in the big paper cups, and they said as follows:

"Feel that sun, hey? Injun summer."

"Mmmm."

"Hey, you know something? I never heard of no guy called Prufrock. You sure that guy pitching's called Prufrock?"

"That's the way it come over the PA system—Prufrock."

"There's a guy around the league what they call Marv *Blay-*lock, or there *was*—and then there's Ike Delock of the Red Sox, a pitcher, y'know, but, man, that fellow out there don't look like no ol' Ike, know whatta mean?"

"You don't suppose it's Shucks Pruett out of Higginsville, Kentucky?"

"No, it ain't Shucks Pruett. Listen. Tell me something. Why do you keep bringing up Shucks Pruett anyway? You got some special thing about Shucks Pruett? He a cousin of yours, or something?"

"I didn't say so. I like the name—that's all. Shucks Pruett. He was a pitcher, y'know, not such a hot one either—for the Phillies back in the late twenties."

"Yeh, yeh, you told me."

They sipped at their beer, and presently, the one with the handkerchief around his neck, the anti-Pruett of the pair, leaned forward and squinted out at the field.

"Hey, you know something?"

"No, what?"

"I'll tell you one thing—Shucks Pruett or no Shucks Pruett— about that guy pitching out there. He's the *palest* pitcher I ever saw. Lookit that face of his—shining out there like a six hundred- watt bulb. You ever see anything like that?"

"Yeh, how 'bout that..."

"Hey, you know something else?"

"No, what?"

"Tell me this. Who's he talking at? He's talking like a house afire out there. You know what I think...I think the sun's affected him, or something."

"You got a point, y'know. Lookit that strange herky-jerky pitchin' motion of his. He looks pretty shook up."

It was true. The physical disintegration had started in while Hodges was at the plate and it progressed quickly. John McGraw once advised a rookie going in to pitch against Honus Wagner: "Chuck the ball as hard as you can...and pray." My trouble was that I had been doing exactly that against *all* the batters from the first. For twenty minutes I had been burning every pitch in, feel- ing that if I let up and tried to guide the ball across the plate the control would vanish utterly. I hadn't bothered to pace myself, and by the time Hodges stood in at the plate I was exhausted. I felt the numbness of it seep through the system like a sea mist. Acutely conscious of the physical self, I fancied I could *see* that engine straining and laboring—the heart crashing and thundering in the rib cage like an overworked pump, the lungs billowing in and out as they whistled heavy warm gouts of air up the long shaft of the throat, and below, the stomach churning and ambulating and wondering why breakfast hadn't been sent down to it that day, or lunch, for that matter, and peeved about it, and then this whole oscillating edifice would tip and sway in the delivery of a pitch, the muscles convoluting and squeaking, off the pitch would go, and then as everything came to a shuddering and wheezing pause at the end of the follow-through, down the long thin corridors and shaftways between the taut tendons would drift that jeering inner voice of mine: "You nut! You fat fool nut! Y'all missed the plate *again!*"

When I finally got the ball over and Hodges lined out his hit, I felt like lying down. My interest in the proceedings was strongly affected by that oncoming dizziness—with its high ringing sound like the mooning hum of a tiny bug caught deep back in the confines of the ear, and while the ball was being fired in by Mickey Mantle in center, I was bent over, puffing hard, and trying to clear my head of its sounds and mists. I could feel the October sun pressing on my neck. When I looked up, Stan Lopata, the Phillies catcher, was settling himself in the batter's box. He has a pronounced crouch at the plate as he awaits the pitch, hunched over as if he'd been seized by a sudden stomach cramp. Naturally, his stance diminishes his strike zone considerably, despite the fact that he's a big man, and I looked down at him in dismay. In fact, my voice, still jeering from the sidelines, produced a perky comment about Lopata which made me smile in spite of myself. "Mah God!" it said. "Lookit what y'all got yo'self into *now*... that's nobody else up there at the plate but Ed Gae*del*... that's who that is, and yo' jes' tell me how y'all gonna pitch to some cat like *that*..."

Ed Gaedel is the name of the famous midget that Zack Taylor, manager of the St. Louis Browns, sent up to bat against a Detroit pitcher named Bob Cain in the first inning of the second game of a doubleheader played in St. Louis in August 1951. The midget had been signed by Bill Veeck, the St. Louis general manager who may have been inspired by James Thurber's short story "You Could Look It Up"—about a minor league manager who in the throes of his team's slump sends in a midget as a pinch hitter. The inner voice didn't dredge up all these facts—just the name Gaedel, and if you looked in at Lopata's coiled stance, crouching there as if he was sneaking up on a bullfrog from behind, you saw how appropriate the choice was: Gaedel measured 3 feet 7 inches and weighed 65 pounds. He came to the plate wearing the number ⅛ on the back of his jersey, swinging three miniature bats, and presented a strike zone which could not have been more than eight inches in height. Since he then adopted a crouching stance—not unlike Lopata's in miniature—the zone must have been shortened to not more than five or six inches. Cain didn't come close with any of his deliveries, and after four balls had sailed over his head Gaedel trotted down to first where an outfielder named Jim Delsing was sent in to run for him. It wasn't his last appearance in a baseball game. After his major league contract was disapproved on the basis that his participation was not in the best interests of baseball, he turned up in a sandlot game in Syracuse, New York. The pitcher wasn't upset by the diminutive strike zone and struck out Gaedel on three called strikes, whereupon the midget turned to the umpire and cried at him shrilly: "You're the worst umpire I ever hope to see."

I threw Lopata four quick balls, wide of the plate, but I wasn't as lucky as pitcher Bob Cain of Detroit. The nightmarish apparition of Ed Gaedel only faced him for the minute or so it took him to issue a walk. But under the special rules of my pitching stint four balls didn't walk a man. You were stuck with him. There was no way by your own action (unless you got three strikes on him, which was unlikely) to get rid of him—as you'd throw out a botched canvas and put a fresh one on the easel—no hope of throwing four quick balls and getting a new batter up there with a stance that was pleasing to the eye: Ted Evans, for example, an English circus giant who offered his dubious services to Bill Veeck after the Gaedel affair—a man who claimed he was 9 feet 3½ inches in height, and who would have had a truly splendid strike zone. No matter how much you willed it, when you looked up, there was Stan Lopata, seemingly as permanent a fixture at the plate as a cast-iron garden sculpture. I threw him fifteen pitches. My mouth was ajar with fatigue, and I was swept by the numbing despair that must grip English bowlers who often have to work on the same pair of batsmen for two or three hours, often more. Lopata and I were a sturdy pair, joined together by the umbilical cord of my wildness—and also by his propensity for hitting fouls. He hit six of them, lashing out like a cobra from his coil, and the ball would flee in big hops down past the coaching boxes or loft into the stands.

"Stan Lopata, next-to-last batter, probably about to hit a foul. He hit an intolerable number of them. My pitching motion has become cramped and stiff from exhaustion." (*Garry Winogrand*)

At this point, Elston Howard, my long-suffering catcher, took a sudden, almost proprietary interest in the proceedings. I think that crouching there in the dust behind home plate he'd counted on his fingers and realized that if we could get Lopata out, there was only one more batter to go, and then he'd be able to walk slowly for the shadows of the dugout, thinking of the slight electric hum of the watercooler and how that stream of cool water would feel against the roof of his mouth, and how he'd flop down on the bench and stick his legs straight out and feel the kinks fade away from them. Previously, his reluctance to enter the spirit of things was such that he could barely persuade himself to lift his glove for a target. Now he began to rise from his crouch after every pitch and fire the ball back with increasing speed— steaming it back trying to snap me out of my wildness. He threw the ball with an accuracy that mocked my control, harder than I was pitching it to him, and finally at such velocity into my weakly padded glove that I suffered a deep bone bruise which discolored my left hand for over a week. "Come on, kid, *lay* it in," I heard him call out once, making a fist of his right hand and pumping it at me as if by sheer determination he could will my pitches into the strike zone. Then he'd crouch down and look gloomily off into the stands, often into his team's dugout, thinking about the water and perhaps to check if relief might be forthcoming, and finally he'd get set and plant his feet in position, and just as you began to swing into the windup he'd pop up the big dusty circumference of his glove fast, as if he was pulling up a target in a shooting gallery. You'd stare at that glove, the eyes watering, concentrating on it so that it seemed to fill the entire field of your vision. But the pitch always seemed to tail off, missing by an inch, perhaps a foot—a moan escaping you as it did—and then you had to face the agony of Howard's return slapping hard enough in the glove to force a sharp intake of breath.

Suddenly the inner voice burst loudly upon my senses. It had been saying nothing of importance—just the usual raillery, still calling me a "fat fool" and an "aggressive nut," but from a distance, hardly distinguishable at times from the high whine of dizziness humming in my ears. But then my hand drifted up and touched my brow, finding it was as wet and cold as the belly of a trout. It was a disclosure which sent the voice spinning off in a cracker-Cassandra's wail of doom. "Mah God!" it cried out. "Y'all gonna *faint* out heah. Lawd *Almah*ty! Y'gonna *faint!*"

I'd just caught the ball from Howard, grimacing as it whacked into the glove, and as I felt the lurch of nausea and that piercing disclosure echo in the brain I dropped the ball from fingers which began bumping gently against each other in a disembodied fashion which suggested that they too had joined the voice in revolt. I stared at the fingers, fascinated. When I bent for the ball, the head cleared slightly, and the fingers came back under control. But I knew then that it was only a matter of time, and not too much of it, before that prescient wail would be proved accurate—and into my mind reeled a terrifying hallucination: the brown canvas of the stretcher I'd seen pegged to the wall in the corridor near the dugout, hands reaching briskly for it, while outside I suddenly seemed suspended far above the field, lofted up there by some such agent as Arthur Larsen's eagle into the high clear air where the stadium pigeons worked the quick currents on dihedral wings, and far below I could see the physical husk of me, deserted now by both mind and eye, stiff-limbed, yet spastic, reeling around the mound trying to pull itself together for that last awful pitch. The crowd was standing now, leaning forward. "You mean to say that guy's Al Schacht?... the clown prince of baseball, *that* guy... well, I don't know what *he* thinks is funny, but I mean that's just terrible, just *hor*rible what's going on out there..." They chatted among themselves, the stretcher-bearers waiting in the runway, smoking cigarettes, and as we watched the grotesque figure shiver into its final windup, the right arm moving as stiffly as an old maid throwing her knitting bag at something scuttling in a dark corner, the ball fell from its feeble grip, hopping slowly down off the mound like an infant rabbit let loose, and after it, plunging forward as if to recapture it, the body lurched and began to collapse to the ground in sections — the head twisting in the dust, then the shoulders, and the knees touching so that, in the jackknifed position of a man looking under a bed for a collar button, the posterior alone remained aloft for one defiant cataleptic instant before it swayed far to one side and toppled in the dust *thump*. We watched the stretcher-bearers flip their cigarettes and start up the steps of the dugouts where the ballplayers stood and rocked back and forth like trolley passengers in their glee, whooping and hollering and giggling at the demise of the impostor: "Man, d'ja see that big tall cat fall *down* out there — hooo-eeee!"

I had one frightening glimpse of my Armageddon, vivid as a lightning flash, and then, waiting, on the mound, the cold sweat standing out in beads that formed as soon as I brushed a finger through them, I tried to persuade myself that you don't collapse out on the pitcher's mound in front of 20,000 people. It isn't done and therefore it couldn't happen. Casey Stengel tells a story of a rookie shortstop who fainted in his debut when the first batted ball hopped out toward him; but that was a question of nerves—if you were to believe the story—not of exhaustion.

But I knew, as I stood there in that momentary calm of self-appraisal, that the energy was draining from me like meal from a punctured burlap sack, and that presently I would stumble and go down like the figure in the vision. It was an inexorable fact. Of course, I could have walked off the field. But calling off the whole thing—just stopping—seemed too complicated. What would happen then? There was no one to finish the job. The American League couldn't bat, therefore. What would Mickey Mantle say? How would the $1,000 be divided? Anything seemed infinitely more complicated than staying. So I became absolutely resigned to continuing, even if it meant falling in a heap, as limp and pale on the mound as a massive rosin bag, while downtown in the magazine offices the editors were told over the phone by someone growling through the thick mesh of a chewed cigar that one of their writers had passed out on the pitcher's mound and the groundskeepers wanted to know what to do about it.

CHAPTER 16

There remained one small hope. If I could last through Lopata and Bill Mazeroski of the Pittsburgh Pirates, the last batter in the National League lineup, I might get a chance while the teams changed sides to puff a bit in the cool of the dugout, to put a wet towel around the back of the neck, and perhaps find a second wind to get through Fox and Mantle and Kuenn and the others in the American League batting order. It was a forlorn hope, and not one to look forward to with eagerness; as soon as I started throwing to Lopata again, the weight of the twenty previous minutes of hard throwing—by then I'd thrown a few pitches short of seventy—pressed down hard like a stifling tropic heat...the field seemed as limitless under that blazing sun as a desert, spreading out forever on all sides, unreal, and the players stiff and distant as obelisks in a surrealist landscape. The whine in my ears increased, the nausea fulminating, the knees rubbery, so shaky that the desert's fixity was disturbed and the ground itself then began to undulate softly and thickly, like a bog, and there were times when the motion became violent and the pitcher's mound hunched up under me so that I teetered on its summit, on the cone of a vast anthill whose slopes beat with that insect hum; at times its physical aspect would be inverted, and I would find myself at the bottom of a murky hollow—the air heavy and clammy—and I would twist and convolute and hurl up the long sides of that bowl a baseball as heavy and malleable as a ripe mango—throwing it up toward Lopata, perched on that distant rim as implacable as a squatting Sphinx.

I don't remember Lopata grounding out, but he did, finally, hitting a big, hopping ground ball toward the shortstop position, where—according to my statistician—Billy Martin first gave a little startled jump as if in surprise to hear the *whack* of the ball being hit, then moved for it on legs that seemed "stiff from disuse," as my statistician friend put it (after all, he'd been standing in his position for some time), and promptly fumbled it. I don't remember that at all.

I don't remember Bill Mazeroski either. I only know I pitched to him that afternoon because my statistician wrote in his notes *Mazeroski at plate...takes,* and then four downward strokes in a row with his pencil to indicate the batter stood with his bat on his shoulder and watched either four or one thousand one hundred and eleven balls go by. When I look at his photographs in the sports magazines, I feel no association, no sense of recognition. Curiously, one of his nicknames is spectral: No Touch, his teammates call him—actually for his great fielding speed, executing the sweep of the ball from the pivot in the double-play so rapidly it hardly seems human hands have been involved in the maneuver. Once, just by chance, passing a television set glowing in a corner during a buffet dinner, I saw the letters M-a-z-e-r-o-s-k-i spelled out in a shaving-soap commercial under a face bulbous with white lather, just his eyes visible above the soap, and I said, "Wait a minute," and dropped down in front of the set. The girl carrying the salad bowl came up behind me and said: "What's wrong...you thinking of changing shaving soaps or something?"

"No, no," I said, looking intently at the screen. "It's that guy doing the commercial behind all that soap...I'm supposed to know him."

"You're supposed to know him?" She knelt down gracefully, setting the salad bowl in front of us on the carpet. "How do you mean you're supposed..."

"What I mean is I should know him," I began to explain. "I was associated with him once — under trying conditions — but I just don't remember..."

The girl leaned forward eagerly. "My God!" she said. "You mean it's sort of like shock therapy: you'll see this guy emerge from all that soap and something'll click and it'll all come back?"

"Something like that," I said.

"It's absolutely terrific," she said.

You never can tell whether she's joking or not. "Now cut it out," I said, "and watch."

Mazeroski had finished his heavy lathering and reached for the razor blade. It was an adjustable razor and we had a close-up of Mazeroski fiddling with it.

A blue-faced cat with large agate eyes, huge-whiskered, was staring out at us from under the set; something apparently moved behind him, for quickly he whirled around with a scrabble of claws in the carpet and tensely inspected the dark corner behind the set; his tail switched back and forth just in front of us; you could sense by the way the girl's hand moved on the carpet that she wanted to reach out and touch that blue tail, but she kept her eyes on Mazeroski's shaving.

"Hey, listen," she said. "I like the way he shaves. Good, firm strokes." She looked at me. "Can you tell yet? Can you recall anything? Any *click?*"

"Cut it out."

"No, it's absolutely thrilling. It's like those drawings coming out — those puzzle-drawings where you follow the numbers with a pencil and suddenly, just like that! you've drawn something: a house, a cocker spaniel . . ."

We watched Mazeroski finish, work a towel briskly over his face, and then, while the commentary on the shaving soap was completed, we had a four- or five-second full-face portrait of him, freshly shaved, a thin, frozen smile on his face which suggested he was holding in some sharp physical hurt, as if down below, out of camera range, some unbearable weight had been placed on his bare feet; as he looked stiffly into the tube of the television camera, beside me the girl kept saying, "Well? Well? Well? Did it work? Did it work?"

"I feel obliged to say," I said, thinking suddenly of the Hiss-Chambers confrontation, "that to the best of my knowledge I've never laid eyes on this man."

"Gee, that's too bad . . . no ringing of bells, or anything?" She seemed genuinely distressed under the helmet of her bamboo haircut. But then she said brightly: "Well, I think you're absolutely nuts — you know that — absolutely blotto . . . I'm not even going to trust you with the salad bowl."

And she didn't either. She picked it up swiftly, looking for the cat as she did so, which had gone, and when we went through the rooms toward the porch where the others waited in the summer evening she walked just a little bit ahead of me and off to one side.

CHAPTER 17

The first definable face that emerged from the thick mist that descended on me when Mazeroski came to the plate was that of Ralph Houk — the tough, confident, chaw-chewing Yankee coach the ballplayers call "Major" for his rank in the Rangers during the war, and who is now Casey Stengel's replacement as the Yankee manager. I was first aware of him when I sensed a movement on the first-base foul line and turned to see him coming toward me. I glowered at him. Whatever his reputation, as he came out over the baseline I looked upon him as an intruder. He came on, a slow nonchalant amble, looking off into the outfield, then down in front of his feet, never at me, and there was no apparent purpose in mind — just a man strolling across the infield — and then he came within the dirt circumference of the pitcher's mound, climbing stiff-legged up toward me, and he put his hand out for the ball.

Perhaps he thought that I'd be relieved to see him. I don't think he expected the belligerency that blazed in that pale face. He shifted the chaw to speak — and I could see a grin working at his mouth. He told me later that he'd relieved many pitchers in his time (he once managed the Denver team in the American Association) but that he'd never seen anyone like that—it was like...well...and with a headshake he'd left the sentence unfinished, as if it all beggared description.

"Needle-lily-eh?"

"What!" I cried at him.

"Need a little help, hey?"

I stared furiously at him.

"Kid, you look a little tired out," he said patiently. "Don't you want some help?" He kept his hand out for the ball.

"No, no, no," I said. My voice came out in a croak. "Gotta finish. Lemme pitch just a li'l more." But Houk didn't turn for the dugout; he smiled, very broadly this time, and kept his hand out.

Like many pitchers, I wasn't taking kindly to being removed—despite being as weak as a convalescent. It's curious that no matter how brutally the opposition is treating him, a pitcher will often turn mulish when the manager reaches the mound. In extreme cases a pitcher will react to the indignity of being relieved by throwing the ball away in a rage. Pitching in Philadelphia, Walter Beck of the Dodgers turned away from his manager, and rather than give up the ball he wound up and hit the Lifebuoy sign with it, which in the old Baker Field was a very long toss from the pitcher's mound indeed. Early Wynn of the Chicago White Sox chose to throw the ball *at* his manager, and threw it into the stomach of Al Lopez, stepping out to relieve him, with such accuracy and dispatch that legend has it that Lopez stumbled back into the dugout murmuring that his star pitcher had shown with his speed and control that he was not in need of relief. The most notable case of an intransigent pitcher involved Boston's Carl Mays, so incensed at being relieved by manager Ed Barrow, and at the Red Sox team in general, that he not only threw the ball into the stands, but jumped the club and vowed he would never pitch for the Red Sox again. Barrow, naturally, suspended him, and after a legal tussle he ended up with the Yankees in New York, where on a fateful day in 1920 in the Polo Grounds (Yankee Stadium hadn't been built) Mays unleashed from his swift swooping subterranean delivery the fastball which on its way over the inside corner of the plate caught Ray Chapman, a notorious plate crowder, paralyzed in this instance, on the side of the head and killed him.

Mays had a disposition well known in the leagues—there were players who thought he had a perpetual toothache—and, while his temper was in no way accountable for the accident, a manager must have thought twice before stepping out to relieve him.

Houk had no such trouble with me. I said "No, no" a few more times, but finally I took a step forward, dropped the ball in his hand, and stumbled off the mound.

I walked slowly toward the first-base dugout. Most of the players in the dugout were standing up, watching me come in, and many of them were grinning. Just as I reached the baseline, behind me Ralph Houk threw a single pitch to Mazeroski which in a sort of final irony, he hit high and lazy to Bob Cerv in left field. Since my back was to the diamond I didn't see the ball caught, but when it was, the players in the field ran for the dugout, streaming by me without a word and clambering down the steps, most of them headed for the watercooler. I was bewildered by that rush of movement past me; I didn't know what was going on until Billy Martin fell into slow step beside me. "Man," he said, smiling broadly, "it's OK...it's over," and I said weakly, "Sure," and went with him into the dugout, where I turned and sagged down on the bench. The *Sports Illustrated* photographer assigned the story leaned into the dugout and took a picture at that moment: in it you see Whitey Ford, the Yankee pitcher, grinning and looking at the figure seated next to him visibly in some stage of shock — the mouth ajar, the eyes staring, the body itself slack and disjointed as if a loosely stuffed bag had been tossed on the bench. Some months later, an elderly English colonel caught a glimpse of that photograph and said the face reminded him of the stunned look of a bagpipe player who had survived the British thrust at Passchendaele in '17. Someone else, with less reference to draw from but plenty of imagination, said no, the face belonged to a man who sees his wife lean out of the sofa during cocktails and inexplicably garrote the family cat with a length of cord. Whichever, I wore a look of bleak horror, and I remember Ford and Martin, who came over and squeezed in beside me, laughing as I sat between them.

"Know something?" said Ford. "We've been making book here in the dugout as to when you'd keel over."

"No kidding," I said weakly.

"Yup. He was sure sweating out there, wasn't he, Billy? Leaking out of him like it was sawdust." He leaned across me, waiting for verification and Martin's comment. He was already grinning in anticipation.

"Sawdust? That was *blood,* man. First time," said Martin, "I ever thought I'd be running in for a mound conference to find

"Flanked by Whitey Ford and the Yankee batboy just after my ordeal. The photograph was snapped as I dropped down between them — providing an accurate study of shock, in my case, and justified amusement from the ballplayers. They were not at all displeased that their profession had treated me as roughly as it had." (*Garry Winogrand*)

out what was going on was a *funeral service*," and he and Ford leaned off the bench and bellowed with laughter that turned heads down the length of the dugout. They wanted to know what Martin had said, and so he said it again, and from down the line they were all looking and grinning. They called up the questions: "Hey, kid, what d'ja think of it, hey? How d'ja like it out there? Pretty rough, hey?"— their joshing friendly, but you could tell they were pleased their profession had treated me as roughly as it had.

"Really sumpin'," I said.

"What'd he say?" someone called out.

"Really *sump*in' out there," I repeated.

While I relaxed, still breathing hard and feeling the true luxury of strength flowing back in, the team sent its first batters up against Ralph Houk. There was a lot of enthusiasm, the players leaning on the dugout steps and shouting encouragement. They stood to divide the $1,000 prize if they could overcome the National League's total of seven points gained off my pitching—four for Thomas's home run, two for Robinson's double, and one for Hodges's single. It was a total substantial enough to invite comment from Martin. He turned to me and said: "That's a lot of *points* you've given those characters with that sneaky slow ball of yours. You a National League fan, hey, kid?... You root for Pittsburgh or something?..."

"Oh gosh, no," I said in dead seriousness. "I was really trying out there."

"*Really trying!* Man, with all that sweat, *dyin'* is the word you're looking for: you were really *dyin'* out there, man..." and he and Ford nearly fell off the bench with glee, whooping and coughing, and finally Martin said weakly, "Man oh *man!*" and headed for the watercooler down in the corner of the dugout. I laughed a bit too, but not as hard.

The general hilarity in the dugout died down rather quickly. Out on the field, in less than five minutes, Houk retired Kuenn, Fox, Mantle, Cerv, Howard, and Malzone—a qualified murderers' row—with simple batting-practice tosses.

It was surprising, and sitting in the dugout you could sense the gloom that came with the frustration of not being able to drive those pitches out of sight. But in actual fact, if you go to the park early and watch batting practice you see that hitting a ball—even if it's tossed easily over the heart of the plate—with power and accuracy is done relatively better by the professionals, but by no means to any degree of perfection. You see them swing and miss in the batting cages; they hit many fouls, their timing perhaps thrown off by the slow speed of the pitch, its arched trajectory incomparable to the clothesline blur of a ball thrown in competition. Lefty Gomez, the Yankee southpaw, on one occasion when he was ahead of the Washington Senators by nine runs, let up, just to see what would happen, and started lobbing his pitches over the plate. After his career, he used to say it was the only time he could remember retiring three batters on three pitches: the first man lined out, the second hit a high long fly to Joe DiMaggio in center, and the third grounded out to Phil Rizzuto at shortstop.

Houk's lucky string was finally broken by the seventh batter, Mickey Vernon, who whacked a drive down the right-field line which pulled all the players on the dugout steps up onto the playing field to watch the ball's flight—all of them yelling at it and applying tortured body English to try to push its trajectory into fair territory, and they let out a great whoop when the ball hit the foul pole for a home run and four points. They slapped Vernon on the back when he came into the dugout, and then hurled their encouragement after Billy Martin, the last man in the order—striding to the plate with their sole chance of copping the prize money resting on his emulating Vernon and picking up four points with a home run. He waited out a few pitches and then swung his bat around viciously and firmly on the ball, but despite that same scramble of body English on the dugout steps, the ball floated straightaway deep into right-center field and was hauled down there by Richie Ashburn. That finished the contest and gave the National League team the *Sports Illustrated* prize seven points to four. One or two of them were grinning as they ran for their dugout across the way. I thought it was as good a time as any to get out of the American League dugout. So I slid off the bench and headed down the runway for the showers.

CHAPTER 18

I didn't see anyone in the locker room. I took off the baseball outfit slowly and sat for a long time in the cubicle looking down at my bare toes, working them up and down, and thinking of nothing, trying to keep the mind blank because when you thought back to what had been going on just minutes before, the excitement began to jitter through you again. Finally I hopped up and went into the shower and stood under a nozzle that malfunctioned and worked in spiteful gusts. The soap in the metal dishes was an astonishing pink color. The dirt I'd scooped up in front of Don Newcombe ran from my hair for the drains in rivulets of red mud. The water was cool. The trainer told me later he hadn't expected anyone to be in the showers so early; after all, he wanted to know, how many pitchers were driven to the showers before the game had even started. But the cool water was pleasant. Under it, luxuriating, I remembered Bruce Pearson, the barely articulate catcher from Mark Harris's great baseball novel *Bang the Drum Slowly*—which our generation thought good enough to make Ring Lardner and the epistolary device of his *You Know Me, Al* cork up and take a backseat when it came to baseball fiction — and I thought of Pearson speculating idly with his teammates about the best moments of baseball...how even hitting a foul ball was part of it, to look up and see how high you drove it, and how the best part of all perhaps was coming in stinking from the sun and ripping off the suit and getting under the shower and thinking about eating. I thought about it because for the first time that day I was suddenly hungry. Roy Campanella once said that you had to have an awful lot of little boy in you to play baseball for a living. So it was, when you recalled it, that the simple, basic sensations came to mind — like being hungry when it was all over, and the sluice of shower water on your arms, and before that, on the field, the warmth of the sun, and the smell of leather, the three-in-one oil sweating out of the glove's pocket in the heat, and the cool of the grass and the dirt when the shade fell across it late in the afternoon, and the sharp cork sounds of the bats against each other, and the rich smell of grass torn by spikes — all these condiments to the purpose, to be sure, which was the game itself, and winning...but still such a part of baseball with the other sounds, and what else you saw, and felt, that finally the actual event itself was eclipsed: the game and its feats and the score became the dry statistics, and what you remembered were the same pressures that once kept you and the others out in the long summer evenings until the fireflies were out and the streetlights shining dimly through the pale-silver underside of leaves, and you groped at the edge of the honeysuckle and threw up that last one high fly for someone to catch and hoped they would see it against that deep sky — and the fact that your team in the brighter hours of the afternoon had lost twenty-four to six and your sister had made eight errors in right field wasn't important. The disasters didn't amount to much. Standing under the shower I found myself thinking not of the trembling misery of the last minutes on the mound, but of Ed Bailey and how he had reared up out of his crouch and given recognition to that roundhouse curve of mine. I thought of those two high flies that Ashburn and Mays hit, how they worked up into that clear sky, and how you knew they were harmless and would be caught. You could be a bona fide pitcher like Hal Kelleher of the Phillies and suffer the indignity of allowing twelve runs in one inning—which he did back in 1938—and in desolation punt your glove around the clubhouse while the trainer stood in a corner pretending to fold towels...and yet that startling statistic was not what Kelleher would remember about baseball. What he *would* remember made you envy him, and all the others that came before and after who were good at it, and you wondered how they could accept quitting when their legs went. Of course, there were a few who didn't feel so strongly. In 1918 a rookie named Harry Heitman walked in for his major league debut with the Brooklyn Dodgers, gave up in succession a single, a triple, and a single...was taken out, went to the clubhouse, showered, left the ballpark for a recruiting station, and enlisted in the United States Navy. To hell with it, he said.

But when I dressed in my street clothes it was with regret that I stuffed the baseball outfit back into the carryall. I found myself looking around the locker room carefully so that I could remember it, not to write about it as much as to convince myself that I had been there. I noticed the red boxes still on the table, filled with baseballs the players had been autographing earlier, and I went over and looked down at them. I had an irresistible urge to sign one of them—perhaps just a scribbled initial. I started looking for a pen. I felt the whole afternoon was slipping away and had to be commemorated, even if by this sad sort of *graffiti*—scratching a name so that there would be evidence, no matter how insignificant, to prove that day. It seemed very important. But the door of the locker room swung open. Some players came in, and I never got the thing done.

When I emerged from the clubhouse into those crowds above, I could feel it slipping away fast. The baseball diamond and the activity of the players, now engaged in their regular game, seemed unfamiliar and removed. Someone smacked a ball which was caught after a long run but the steel pillars cut my view and I couldn't distinguish either of the participants in the play. No one recognized me as the *Sports Illustrated* pitcher as I went down the aisles looking for an empty seat. The lower stands were crowded and I turned and headed up the ramps and finally found a seat at the top of the stadium in the upper deck. I flagged down a hot-dog vendor, and behind him the beer vendor, and far below on the field Willie Mays stole a base as the crowd roared. Over the rumpus of noise I heard the prying voice of an usher. He was leaning in from the aisle, demanding: "Hey, chief—gotcha ticket sub?"

I had just paid for two hot dogs and was at that moment handing the beer vendor his money, the focal point of a congestion that then included the two vendors, the usher who wanted to see my ticket, and behind him, carrying a red thermos jug, a worried-looking man in whose seat I was obviously sitting.

"You mean my ticket?" I said, stalling for time, wondering how I could announce with any authority to that group that I'd legally entered the stadium by the players' gate.

"What's this—the upper deck?" I said, looking around. "I must be up here too high. I think I belong lower down—in the mezzanine," and I peered around aggrieved, as if some other agency than my own legs had deposited me there.

I went back down the ramps with my hot dogs and the beer looking for another seat—in a limbo state of being neither ballplayer nor spectator—as nomadic as the youngsters who scuttle in without paying and are flushed like shorebirds and flutter down two or three sections to settle again until the ushers come down the aisles with their big dusting mittens.

I went down to the lower grandstand to the field box where Toots Shor was sitting with his family. There weren't any extra seats so I crouched briefly in the aisle. Shor looked around. "You're outa condition," he said. "Whassamatter? At your age I could've pitched to ten dozen of those crumbums." He leaned out and pushed a jab into my rib cage. "But what the hell," he said. He turned back to the playing field. Billy Martin was in the on-deck circle and Toots shouted at him: "Hey, Billy!" Martin was dusting the bat handle with the rosin bag. Toots shouted again: "Hey, *Billy!*" over the hum of the crowd, turning heads by the score in our vicinity, and Martin looked around. "Smack it, kid!" Toots shouted. Martin indicated with a shrug he couldn't hear over the crowd noise. Toots lifted himself out of this seat. "I said *smack it!*" he bellowed. He made a ferocious gesture with his arm to illustrate what he meant, and Martin nodded and went back to dusting his bat with the rosin bag.

I remembered it afterward, very clearly—crouched before Shor, working on the second hot dog, and watching his neck bulge with that effort of communication: I thought what a long way it was out there over those box railings — not only a distance to shout across, but so remote and exclusive that it seemed absurd and improbable that I had been out there. It all seemed not to have happened, and later, tired of my wanderings, when I tried to explain to a sympathetic-looking usher who finally gave me a seat why I didn't have a ticket, I couldn't seem to do it with much conviction. I kept my voice low talking to him to keep anyone else from overhearing.

But I had the reality for a while. Even late that afternoon, when the game was over, I had yet to sink into the true anonymity of the spectator. At the last out I watched the kids leap over the box railings and run for the pitcher's mound. Baseball finished for the season, the stadium guards didn't bother to throw their protective cordon around the infield. The youngsters' high

Curious youngsters peer into the dugout for a glimpse of their heroes. (*Garry Winogrand*)

cries drifted back into the stands: *Hey, lookit, lookit me, I'm Whitey Fawd*—and they jostled each other for the chance to toe the rubber and fling imaginary fireballs to imaginary catchers. The gates were opened and the spectators began to file onto the field, headed for the exits in deep center field. Many of them stopped and stood on the top steps of the dugout, and stared at the empty wooden benches. But I didn't go down on the field— not that day, at least. I knew I'd been out there. So I left the stadium by the ramps behind the stands.

About the Author

George Plimpton (1927–2003) was the bestselling author and editor of more than thirty books, as well as editor of the *Paris Review* for its first fifty years. He wrote regularly for such magazines as *Sports Illustrated* and *Esquire,* and he appeared numerous times in films and on television.